W9-AMM-498

God Rest Ye Grumpy Scroogeymen

God Rest Ye Grumpy Scroogeymen

New Traditions
for Comfort & Joy at Christmas

Laura Jensen Walker
& Michael K. Walker

Fleming H. Revell
A Division of Baker Book House Co
Grand Rapids, Michigan 49516

© 2003 by Laura Jensen Walker and Michael K. Walker

Published by Fleming H. Revell
a division of Baker Book House Company
P.O. Box 6287, Grand Rapids, MI 49516-6287

Printed in the United States of America

All rights reserved. No part of this publication may be reproduced, stored in a retrieval system, or transmitted in any form or by any means—for example, electronic, photocopy, recording—without the prior written permission of the publisher. The only exception is brief quotations in printed reviews.

Library of Congress Cataloging-in-Publication Data
Walker, Laura Jensen.
    God rest ye grumpy scroogeymen / Laura Jensen Walker and Michael K. Walker.
        p.   cm.
    Includes bibliographical references.
    ISBN 0-8007-1834-8
    1. Christmas. I. Walker, Michael K. II. Title.
GT4985.W285   2003
394.2663—dc21   2003007031

Unless otherwise indicated, Scripture is taken from the HOLY BIBLE, NEW INTERNATIONAL VERSION®. NIV®. Copyright © 1973, 1978, 1984 by International Bible Society. Used by permission of Zondervan. All rights reserved.

Scripture marked KJV is taken from the King James Version of the Bible.

Michael: For my family, from Grandma Adelaide all the way down to our newest member, Lexi. I love you.

Laura: For my family, with love, and especially in remembrance of my beloved Grandma Florence, who filled my Wisconsin childhood with such sweet Christmas memories.

And for Lonnie, who first had the idea for this book. Dear friend, wonderful editor, and fellow rabid cinemaphile who had never seen *A Christmas Story* until this past Fourth of July. Here's lookin' at you, kid.

Contents

Research shows that nobody ever reads introductions to books, so this is the first chapter. Really.

1

Not Really an Introduction

People *never* bother to read the introductions to books—(c'mon, be honest. Do you?)—they go straight to the first chapter. Therefore, to make sure we got your attention from the first page, we decided to skip an introduction and dive right in.

So hang onto your stockings, holiday reader, and join us on our merry Yuletide journey.

In the spirit of the season, we wanted to offer an alternative to the usual holiday opus—to show you that, single or married, with or without kids, you can still find ways to make the season bright. And because we believe as Charles Dickens did that it's important to "honor Christmas in my heart, and try to keep it all the year."

We love Christmas. Pretty much everything about it, too.

One holiday season some friends of ours decided not to put up a Christmas tree, lights, or any decorations. After all, it was just the two of them—no kids—so why bother?

Why indeed!

Even though it's just the two of us and Gracie, our dog, we still decorate.

It's a tradition.

Traditions are important to our health and well-being. As well as helping us know how we fit in to a given special day or season, they help us through the hard times. When our roads turn rocky and life is uncertain, there is comfort and continuity in doing things the way we always do them.

Sometimes our friends—even the ones who regularly visit our home—marvel at the amount of "stuff" we put out at Christmas.

It's true. We do have a lot of decorations. But it's much more than just "stuff."

It's memories. Reminders of years and decades past.

The Nativity scene Michael's mother made for him. The artificial tree she and Michael's sister bought in the mid-1970s—it *still* looks great when decorated. The hand-carved wooden ornaments from Laura's Air Force days in Germany.

Then there are the years we've shared together as well. Moments that may have been forgotten were it not for the memento.

Each year as we unpack our Christmas boxes, we are reminded of our history and our heritage.

One friend confided that she really wanted to celebrate the season but just didn't know how, or where to begin.

In these pages, we're each going to talk—sometimes Michael, sometimes Laura, sometimes both of us—and we're going to offer you some practical tips and share our stories, successes, and more. (Just wait till you get to some of the recipes. Yumm!) It is our desire to inspire you to see December from a slightly different vantage point. Whether you more resemble a Grinch or one of the Magi from the East, our hope is that this book will help you increase your celebration, internally and eternally.

Every newlywed feels the clash: "That's not the way *my* family does it." And so the traditions change. Whether it's doing things the way your spouse always did them growing up or deciding on new ways to celebrate, your traditions are an amalgam of who you are and from whence you came.

Something that is common to both of us is our love of movies. It's one of the things that first drew us together. Therefore, you are going to find a lot of movie references in this book—beginning here.

While much of the holiday season is focused around "things," there's a great line in the original *Miracle on 34th Street* where Kris Kringle is talking to the young

Alfred, who says, in that great New York accent, something like, "Yeah, there are a lot of bad 'isms' in the world, but the woist is commoicialism."

While it may sound strange, you can still have a lot of stuff yet avoid the spirit of commercialism.

We do.

We don't find it necessary to run around *buying* more and more stuff. Instead, we like to be creative and make things at home—even pulling last-minute gifts together from things we have on hand—baskets, books, baked goods, and the like.

Keep in mind that Christmas is so much more than just a tree, decorations, the pageant at church, lots of shopping, and—ugh—fruitcake. Christmas celebrates the birth of the one who came to give us new life. And as we remember that, we are blessed.

> He lies in a manger.
> Ruler of the stars,
> He nurses at his mother's breast.
> He is both great in the nature of God,
> And small in the form of a servant.
>
> Augustine of Hippo

She wants elegance; he wants fun. She likes white lights that cast a steady, silvery glow; he likes colored ones that blink on and off.

2

His 'n Her Christmas Trees

Selfishness makes Christmas a burden;
love makes it a delight.

Author Unknown

I t was a typical newlywed dilemma. She squeezed the middle; he neatly rolled the end of the tube. She liked Aquafresh; he didn't.

But creative problem solver Michael quickly fixed this bathroom conundrum. He bought a second tube of toothpaste.

His 'n hers. All is well.

We ran into the same problem at the holidays. Our very first Christmas together as husband and wife, we were living in a tiny apartment without a whole lot of decorating room. So we bought an artificial tabletop Christmas tree.

One late November day while I was out grocery shopping, Michael decided to surprise me by putting up the tree and beginning the decorating.

I walked in the door, when what to my wondering eyes should appear but colored tree lights blinking Christmas cheer and a construction paper–chain garland looped 'round the branches. As my eyes traveled upward, I beheld clumps of thick, flashy gold garland draped above the window.

I was a bit taken aback because I've always been more of a simple, non-blinking white lights kind of gal myself. And strands of shimmery pearls were my garland of choice:

"Oh. You've put up the tree," I said brightly.

"Yep," he beamed, looking up from his box of ornaments on the floor. "Surprised?"

"Definitely."

My darling helped me put the groceries away, and in an attempt to get into the Christmas spirit, I made us mugs of hot chocolate with mini marshmallows as we nestled in among our boxes of ornaments.

From his box, Michael eagerly pulled out Mickey Mouse, Charlie Brown, and other colorful plastic cartoon characters, along with lots of reindeer, snowmen, and fat Santa dough ornaments that he'd hand painted.

Meanwhile, I carefully unwrapped delicate glass balls; dainty white porcelain trinkets in the shape of

14

teacups, angels, and hearts; and a variety of other silver and gold, often lacy, Victorian-style baubles.

Warning! Warning! as the robot on *Lost in Space* used to say. Taste collision! Taste collision!

Pretty soon we realized that between the two of us we had way too many ornaments for our little tree. So we democratically decided that we'd each pick our top fifteen or so to use. When we finished trimming the tree that night, there was Mickey snuggled up next to my favorite pink and white rose-patterned teacup, while Snoopy, in all his primary-colored Christmas finery, made eyes at my pretty gold-and-lace angel.

It was a sight to behold.

The next day when Michael got home from work, Mickey, the Peanuts gang, and most of their little cartoon friends had mysteriously made their way to the back of the tree—encircled by the paper chain garland.

The front of the tree was a thing of beauty with its symmetrically looped strings of white pearls gleaming behind a host of silver and gold Victorian ornaments.

But for some reason, Michael wasn't happy with this new arrangement.

"You *hate* all my ornaments, don't you?" he asked.

"Of course not, honey! It's just that I thought it looked better to group all the bright primary-colored ones together in one area and the pretty, uh, I mean 'girly,' ones in another area. Besides," I pointed to the far right side of the tree, "I kept your favorite Charlie Brown ornament in front."

The following year when we were living in a larger place, we invested in his 'n her trees—at Michael's suggestion.

Now we were both happy Christmas campers.

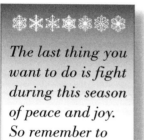

The last thing you want to do is fight during this season of peace and joy. So remember to focus on ways to reduce your stress—rather than adding to it—and enjoy the season instead.

I got my elegant Victorian tree with white lights and pearls in the living room, and Michael got his fun multicolored kid-style tree in the den.

Then there was the time Michael came home with a plastic revolving color-wheel light. If you're over forty, you know what I'm talking about. The plug-in-the-wall dealy-bob with the four triangular pieces of hard plastic—red, green, blue, and amber—in front of a flood lamp that casts its rotating colors onto the tree. Very popular in the 1960s.

When he pulled it from the box to proudly show me, I said, "That's hideous and you're not bringing it into my house."

"But it was only three bucks at a yard sale," he protested. "Besides, I always wanted one when I was a kid."

"We *had* one when I was a kid and used it on our white flocked Christmas tree. But that doesn't make it any less tacky."

"Well, I'm keeping it and using it on *my* tree!"

And he did. That year, anyway. Every year since, he takes it down out of the garage rafters and pretends he's going to use it—until I notice. Then he smiles and puts it back in the garage until the next year.

Over the course of our marriage, what initially started out as his 'n hers has now evolved into "ours." "My" tree is now "our Victorian tree," and "his" tree is "our fun tree."

I've let down my snob guard and am now much more open to mixing and matching ornaments from both trees, and to injecting a little more fun, rather than *House Beautiful* elegance, into our home at the holidays.

Case in point: Michael never had a train set as a child—and, like most boys, had always wanted one—so a few years ago when he found a small one on sale at our local hardware store, he excitedly brought it home.

Tree Trimming Tip

Try using something unconventional to decorate your tree. For instance, our Victorian tree sports some little-girl toy china teacups and an occasional lace doily draped over a branch. The pearl garland on that tree inspired the garland on the fun tree: Michael's mother's brightly colored bead necklaces clasped together. We received them after his mom passed away—still in the wooden jewelry box he'd made for her in ninth-grade shop class.

He automatically began to carry it into the den to set it up around the base of the fun tree, but I stopped him in his tracks.

"Honey, why don't you set it up here in the living room?"

"Under *your* tree—I mean, the Victorian tree?" he said incredulously.

"Yes. I think it would be perfect."

I've mellowed over the years.

Although I must confess, Mickey has still never set foot on the Victorian tree.

3

Of craft fairs and homemade ornaments.

Here We Come A-Handcrafting

Joy is a net of love by which we can capture souls. . . . God loves the person who gives with joy. Whoever gives with joy gives more.

Mother Teresa

Ask any mom or grandma, often it's the handcrafted gifts that mean the most.

Or ask any big sister for that matter. My (Michael's) sister Debbie still has the paper holder I made way back in ninth-grade shop class. The cheesy one of the duck cut out of wood with a clothespin for a beak. Tilt its head back to open its mouth and release the papers.

No matter how many times Debbie moves, it still has a place next to her computer.

Then there's the white porcelain jaybird perched atop the shelf in our den. My grandmother gave it to us, and it's especially beautiful to me because it was made by her sister.

The list could go on and on. Even when it's not made by someone we know, there's still something extra special about items crafted by hand.

I have to admit that God has gifted me when it comes to crafting ability. Our home has many examples of my handiwork—as do the homes of our families and friends. But as I get older, the responsibilities of life continue to encroach upon my free time—and the family just keeps on getting bigger.

I started making quilts—yes, this is Michael talking. I'm one of the minority who can say with political correctness that my quilts are "man-made." Anyway, I started making quilts for the various parents and siblings and then began working my way through the nieces and nephews. But our nieces and nephews keep having more great-nieces and great-nephews! And there's just not enough time to keep up with all the baby quilts. I'm currently so far behind I may never die.

So I often stick to smaller, less complicated projects.

There are tons of craft magazines and craft programs on TV that offer great ideas for things to make. They're often designed for beginning skill levels, so almost anyone can make gifts. Okay, okay. Notice I did say "almost."

My sweetie has quite a gift for arranging and decorating—her magazine-fanning technique is well known in many circles, and her knickknack angling ranks with the best. But even she will admit that she's not very "crafty" when it comes to *making* decorative items.

Yet she's eager to take home-court advantage of *my* skills. When we were newly married, she thought that any occasion was appropriate for my making a quilt.

"My cousin's friend's son in Wisconsin is getting married. Do you think you might be able to whip out a quilt for them as a present?"

Those requests abruptly died the year Laura asked me to "whip out" a set of placemats for our friends Pat and Ken.

"Nothing fancy, honey. Just little rectangular quilts in Christmas colors that they can put plates of food on . . . And can you make a set of eight, sweetie?"

"Sure. But think you can help me by making some matching napkins, my love?"

"Of course, darling. Just show me what to do."

Well, *I* cut and marked the fabric, so all she needed to do was iron and hem the four sides of the napkins.

Can you say bored? Out of her skull?

It was so monotonous—and warm—to iron all those straight lines, and then *sew* all those straight lines. (My beloved hates to sew.) And for what? You can buy the silly things at Wal-Mart for two bucks.

The great thing was that Laura realized that hers was not that big of a job compared to piecing the rectangle tops, adding the batting and backing, and finishing the placemats.

21

I never did let on that it was a setup. Well, not until the day I wrote this chapter, anyway. And it very successfully showed her that there's really no such thing as "whipping out" a quilt. Thankfully, it also greatly reduced the requests for my making quilts for people we've only just met.

Instead, we shifted to little projects.

One idea for great homemade gifts is Christmas ornaments. Whether they are the presents themselves or an extra special gift wrap decoration, ornaments are great. In fact, I've been making and giving them for years. Each year I have a tradition of making a special ornament. I usually write the name of the recipient and the year on each. The oldest one with my name on it is a bread-dough bell, shaped by a cookie cutter, painted red with green trim. It's dated 1979.

Sometimes the ornaments are very simple—like the first year Laura and I attended the *Nutcracker Ballet* together. I cut the colorful pictures off the program covers, glued them to poster board and hung them from golden ribbon. Our names and the year are written in calligraphy on the back as a reminder of this special occasion.

Other ornaments are more complicated—like the "chemo ball" ornaments. Let me explain.

The day after our first wedding anniversary, Laura was diagnosed with breast cancer. Part of her treatment was done at home. The chemotherapy—and her reaction to it—was so severe that she had to be on intravenous fluids for the week after her treatments. But at least she could be at home.

I changed her IV bags and even gave her shots. And I would administer her anti-nausea medication—which came in a plastic container—via her IV. Maybe because it was autumn, or maybe because I'm just demented, I noticed that the casing sort of resembled an ornament. A little smaller than a baseball and slightly elongated, it was conveniently hanging from its own string, er, plastic tubing. I mentioned this to Laura, but she didn't think it amusing. Because of the nausea, it took her days after each treatment to be able to eat anything. That "thing" I was dangling in front of her was to keep her from retching, not for decorating at Christmas.

But a plan began forming in my mind.

I thought about the stories in the Old Testament where the children of Israel did things as mementoes for the future. The Passover celebration is full of these mementoes. We eat this to remember such and such. When you see this, remember this or that. Holy Communion is the same type of thing: "Do this in remembrance of me." Knowing that the cancer was a turning point in our lives, one of those things that irrevocably changes us, I determined to make a tribute to remind us of it. In a very small way, like the Passover celebration. To remind us of something from which the Lord had delivered us.

When I mentioned making Christmas ornaments out of the chemo balls, Laura was incredulous. "No way! You're not going to hang that on the tree! You're sick!"

Which may be the truth, but I could envision what it would *become* when completed. She saw only a piece of

IV tube and the plastic ball that held the stuff to keep her from throwing up. She wanted no reminder of that. But in my mind's eye, I saw it completed, as an object of beauty.

Kind of the way God sees us. I saw it not as it was, but as it could and would be.

Everyone in the "inner circle" of our lives that year received one of these chemo-ball ornaments for Christmas. Each was beautifully decorated and bore the recipient's name and the year. Laura's was decorated especially for our Victorian tree, painted white with pearls and eyelet lace and swoops of ribbon. Mine was decorated for the fun tree with chubby dancing Santas

For a few years, Laura insisted hers hang on the back of the tree. While she agreed it was beautiful, it was still too painful to bring forward. Then slowly it worked its way toward the front of the tree, a little bit at a time, year by year. The year Laura's book *Thanks for the Mammogram!* came out, we agreed that the ornament deserved to be front and center.

My sister Sheri makes it a point to display her ornament every Christmas. Even during those years when her family decides to do something different and not put out any of the regular decorations, the chemo ball makes it onto the tree.

One of the most wonderful things about our collection of ornaments is the memories. Good times and bad, happy times and sad.

And then there are all of the other gifts we've made and given, or been given. We've given several quilted wall hangings and things I've made in my workshop.

Baskets of Goodies

A lovely and inexpensive gift to give is a basket of a few of your—or rather, the gift recipient's—favorite things, whether it's bath salts, tea and biscuits, cookies, or candy. One year we gave baskets of gourmet spaghetti sauce, colored Christmas tree pasta, and breadsticks for a delicious edible gift to all of our brothers- and sisters-in-law.

Another wonderful idea is to mix up the dry ingredients of your favorite cookie mix in a Mason jar, with a pretty piece of fabric ruffled out of the lid, then attach the recipe to the jar with a pretty ribbon.

One year, a friend found himself with an extra scroll saw. Promising I would use it a lot to make all kinds of things, I persuaded Laura to buy it for me as an early Christmas present. Later that month we gave a wonderful cutout of Joseph and Mary with the baby Jesus in the stable to Pat and Ken, the couple who sold us the saw.

The next November I noticed my scroll saw in the garage and remembered my comments about how much I would use this toy—I mean tool. I also realized that I hadn't turned it on in almost a year. Thinking quickly, I grabbed some pieces of pine and some patterns I'd found long ago. I whipped out another Nativity scene. This time in a "primitive" style that I would be able to paint quickly. After all the sanding, marking of the lines, and painting, I realized this was not something to be mass produced. I didn't remember painting taking so much time. But it was a beautiful Nativity scene, and my grandmother appreciated it so much when she unwrapped it on Christmas Day.

So the saw continues to collect dust. As do my many other tools. But one day I will use them again.

You don't have to have power tools to make beautiful presents.

My brother Bill has a gift idea he's used for several of us—photo collages of family members. Frames with precut mats are available from craft stores and some department stores, all ready for you to add your own photos. A great, thoughtful gift.

Among our dearest possessions are the things made by loved ones.

Laura's father was a gifted painter. We have the unfinished painting he was working on when he died—a portrait of Laura's grandfather. As special as this is, my favorite of his works is the one hanging in her mom's living room—an oil painting of buildings overlooking a canal. While it looks like it might be Venice, it's actually in Belgium. A winter scene with leafless trees and reflections in the nearly still water.

One year for Christmas we received a copy of the painting—a photograph printed onto canvas using a special process. We now have Belgium, and a part of Laura's dad, hanging over our fireplace.

Speaking of photos, my other brother Bob has them down to a science. Literally. The historian in the family,

Bob has spent countless hours researching and gathering photos and documents from our family's history. He used to take these to the office supply store to make laser copies for all of us. With his scanner and printer, and a bit of know-how, he now does it all at home. And we are the recipients of great photos and booklets of our heritage.

But again, you don't need to have a lot of electronic accessories to make wonderful gifts.

I have a treasure dated Christmas 1992. A very simple-looking booklet made for me by Laura when she was too sick to go shopping in the stores. That was the year of the cancer, and Laura's immune system was so compromised by the chemotherapy that she could rarely go out in public—let alone have the energy to walk very far. But she's always been one to look at what she *can* do rather than feeling limited by what she *can't* do. Writer that she is, she made me a booklet and filled it with special messages, the revised lyrics to a special song, a poem, and some quotes especially appropriate to us that year.

What a treasure—the booklet and the one who gave it to me.

So much nicer than socks or a tie.

27

Handcrafting Tip

Even if you are not used to making your own items, visit your local craft store. Don't be intimidated; just do it. They're sure to have kits even the beginner and those with very little time to spare can complete and enjoy. If you don't feel you can finish it by this Christmas, February is a great month to tinker while watching TV or a video.

Or if you don't have the time or inclination to make your own, visit a craft fair and support a local artist. Buy someone else's handiwork. They will appreciate it, as will the recipient of the gift.

Just because your family's always done it that way doesn't necessarily mean it's the only way.

Making New Traditions, Breaking Old Traditions

Habit with him was all the test
of truth;
"It must be right: I've done it
from my youth."

George Crabbe (1754–1832)

My (Michael's) strongest tradition memory is that we got to open one present, and one present only, on Christmas Eve. And Mom got to pick which one.

Pajamas.

Yippie. Yahoo. Just what every kid dreams of.

And we couldn't even pretend we were surprised. Mom had her tradition of always wrapping them the same way. Rolled up in a tube like a sausage, ribbon tying off each end, and the edges of the paper ruffled out like a giant piece of hard candy. I used to dream maybe this year it *would* be candy.

But alas, pajamas were the tradition. That's just the way it was done.

While we kept the opening-one-gift-on-Christmas-Eve tradition, I'm happy to say that somewhere along the line the pajama part faded away.

As did the four o'clock in the morning thing.

Every year one of us six kids would wake up before dawn and wake the rest of the family, and we'd start the wrapping paper–ripping frenzy. Ahhh. Christmas.

All grown up now with families of our own, we've all changed and adapted these traditions to fit our individual family styles. This predawn ritual was one of the first things my sister Sheri changed after she had the twins, Kari and Jennie. "Don't wake up Mom and Dad until after eight o'clock under penalty of death. Or worse, we'll throw away all your new toys."

When the girls were about nine or so, I stayed over on Christmas Eve. My bed for the night—a.k.a. the couch—was situated between the kids' room and the tree. Sure enough, at about a quarter to eight I heard little voices in the hallway.

I pretended to be asleep—still too early, you know. Looking at the tree, and the bounty thereunder, one of them elbowed the other. "*Don't* wake up Mika Mike!"

(As toddlers, they couldn't say, "Uncle." They said, "Mika," and it stuck. And they *still* call me Mika Mike today—now that they're in their twenties.)

Pretending no more, I let them know that I, too, couldn't wait for Christmas to start. The eight o'clock tradition was broken that year.

Laura and I have never held to any specific time-to-wake-up tradition.

But since ours was a whirlwind courtship, our first Christmas together was *after* the wedding—we met in January and married in August. So we learned about many of the other's family traditions as the season progressed. One of the big surprises for Laura was my family's passion for stocking stuffers. The first—and only—clue arrived on Christmas morning.

Stockings in her family were a nice little addition to the gifts under the tree. Some pencils, a new toothbrush, a few tidbits of this and that, candy, and maybe some nuts or a piece of fruit. And she filled my stocking accordingly.

Not so with my family. We're talking major time and investment.

Christmas morning, Laura stared at her stocking in disbelief. I had made her a new one that year, tastefully oversized, Victorian style, emerald green satin, outlined with miniature pearls, and trimmed with a garland of rosebud ribbon. Fully lined for extra strength, of course.

She gasped when she saw it and was amazed at how much I could stuff into it! The new Amy Grant CD, perfume, a couple pairs of earrings, bath salts, oils, miniature soaps, and of course, the requisite office supplies. This in addition to the chocolates, teas, tea biscuits, and the candy cane sticking out the top.

Plus, most important of all, the tangerine in the toe.

Mom always put a tangerine in the toe. As kids we rarely even ate the things, sticking them back in the fridge for someone else to eat later. Even so, not having one in the toe of my stocking was unimaginable.

Until I forgot to mention this to Laura.

I don't remember what *was* in the toe of my stocking that first Christmas, but it was not small, round, and orange.

My poor darling was indeed surprised to learn about my stocking fetish. And she was shocked to learn that I am conservative when compared to some of my siblings. They make me look like Ebenezer Scrooge—before the ghosts.

My sister Debbie even goes so far as to say, "I don't need *any*thing under the tree, but you'd better not forget my stocking!"

When Debbie remarried two years ago, her new husband, Mike, thought he understood this as their first Christmas approached. Debbie's grown children—individually—even took him aside to warn him. So he went out and got her about seven things to open in her stocking and thought he was doing pretty good.

Wrong.

I guess you have to experience my family and their stockings to fully comprehend. Last year he knew—and did it right. This year I've heard rumors about using pantyhose for a stocking so there's extra leg room.

Speaking of siblings, a couple years ago Laura and I finished up all our holiday preparations early. This meant we had time to relax and enjoy the week before Christmas. Early one Friday evening, we thought it would be fun to spend time with family. On impulse we invited my brother Bob and his wife, Debbie, to see the new Sandra Bullock comedy with us. Bob had a meeting that night, and as much as Debbie wanted and *needed* to get away, she had the stocking stuffers to wrap. Undaunted, we suggested she bring everything over to our house; the three of us would make light work of the wrapping and then still have time for the film.

Good thing there was a late showing that night.

She had goodies for Bob, their three sons, one daughter-in-law, two grandchildren, and the few other teens who, while not related by blood or marriage, were still part of the family. The trunk of her car was stuffed full with brown paper grocery bags. One bag per person. "It's the only way I know to keep it all organized," she explained. Okay, so each bag was only a third of the way full. But still . . .

No wonder she felt overwhelmed by the task of wrapping all this stuff.

Especially since *every* item had to be wrapped.

Laura was incredulous. "Not every pencil?"

"Of course every pencil!"

Cranking up some festive tunes on the stereo, the three of us went to work. Even with the mass-production assembly line, it still took a couple of wonderful hours. And we made it to the theater just in time for the 10:00 showing. I think all the laughter and camaraderie throughout the evening made the movie that much more enjoyable. In my memory, Sandra Bullock had never been so funny.

My sister-in-law never did fit all the goodies into the stockings. Some of the stuff always ends up under the tree. But it was great for Laura to put me into perspective. Compared to them, I'm tame.

And Laura and I have come to a happy compromise on our own stockings. Each year we agree on a spending limit. The limit changes each year according to the circumstances, but now we're in line with one another.

Although the tangerine thing is still a stumper at times.

Because I do most of the fruit shopping, Laura tends to stick to the basics. If it's small, round, and orange, it must be a tangerine, right? Even if it's not small, or round, or orange. One year my tangerine was really an apple. But it was in the toe—that should count for something.

A rose by any other name . . .

Traditions are great. They give meaning to our lives, help us know how we fit in, and give us something to look forward to. They're comforting—we know what to expect.

But they should *add* to the celebration, not make us prisoners of the celebration.

"The Year of the Apple" was a great reminder of this lesson. We were out of tangerines, and the grocery store would have been a madhouse on Christmas Eve. Rather than stress out, Laura modified the tradition that year.

When circumstances change, we have the choice of keeping the old traditions or making new ones. Obviously, getting married is one of these times. But so it goes for parents when their children move out of the house. Or for those who find themselves alone due to death, divorce, job relocation, or whatever reason. There are still traditions you can keep or create.

Our friends Curt and Peggy have incorporated a tradition into their family that started in Curt's family when he was a child.

"After Christmas, when all the decorations were being put away, little Curt would write a note to himself and stick it in his stocking so he could read it the following year when the stockings were unpacked," Peggy related. "We began having our boys, Ryan and Don, do that when they were young.

>
> ## Christmas in July?
>
> *Of course! It's a great excuse for a party—with a twist. Time to pull out your Hawaiian shirts and dust off your Christmas CDs. Invite a few choice friends or a whole houseful over and celebrate!*
>
> *Any of the Christmas games can be adapted, and while it might be too hot to cook or bake some of those Christmas recipes, you can always barbecue. After all, even Santa likes a good burger or hot dog.*

"The note might include hobbies they were interested in at the time, things that were going on at school, maybe a little picture they drew, and plans for the coming year. Curt and I joined in this, too, and even to this day, while I am putting away the Christmas things, I will write a note in each person's stocking. It's fun to read and share these when the Christmas things are brought out each year."

My boss, Kendra, has a great "paper" tradition, too. She and her husband each have trinket-box ornaments hanging on the tree, and every year they fold up a little something and put it in each other's ornaments. It could be a gift certificate, movie passes, or concert tickets. Whatever. But this is the very *last* gift they open.

"And every year I forget about the ornaments," Kendra says. "We unwrap all the presents under the tree, and I think we're done. Derek has to remind me that there's one more left, and then it's like an added bonus."

Christmas encore, I'd say, performer that I am.

When I was single, working for a Christian theater company, November and December were naturally our busiest months of the year. The constant giving of ourselves was rewarding but exhausting. Of course, this season is when all the good movies open, and we did not have time to see any. But we didn't work on Christmas Eve or Christmas Day, so these days became our movie marathons. Most of us did not have family in the area—except for each other—so it worked out quite nicely. One year I saw two movies on the 24th and *three* on the 25th.

Now *that* was a tradition.

Moving back to California, I tried to keep a bit of this tradition alive. Laura—a huge movie buff—and I even managed it the first year we were married. But with family on both sides here in town, it became too difficult to fit in every year.

However, we have managed it on occasion. Although we have had to learn to be a little discreet.

Every family has a secret language or special code words that mean something only to them. Well, we've decided that "nap" is code for "matinee." So on Christmas Day we simply tell family that we're really tired and think we'll head out so we can take a nap and that we'll be back for supper.

But, shhhh. It's a secret. Don't tell anyone. This year we're hoping to nap again.

Tradition Tips

Throughout this book we'll be sharing many of our traditions with you. Goodness knows we have plenty of them. But we try not to get so locked into the tradition that we forget to have fun. If your tradition only adds stress and no joy, can you live without it—at least for this year?

Or is there something you've always wanted to try but never have? Why not give it a go this year? Even if your "tradition" is to do something new and different every year! That's a great tradition.

The tantalizing tastes and aromas of the season.

5

O Come All Ye Fruitcakes

Never eat more than you can lift.

Miss Piggy

I (Laura) hate fruitcake.

And most of the world feels the same way.

Okay, maybe that's too sweeping a statement for some of you fruitcake lovers—it's difficult for me to even put those two words in the same sentence (fruitcake LOVERS)—so I'll modify it a little.

I hate fruitcake.

And I submit that the world is divided into two kinds of people: those who like fruitcake—and send it to everyone on their Christmas list each year—and those who hate this dark, heavy, sticky slab of "sweetness" and recycle it to someone else who likes hard, dry, and inedible "pastry" with—yuck!—gelatinous fruit and nuts squished inside.

I may hate fruitcake, but I love almost every other food associated with Christmas. Especially those with a smidge—or gallon—of chocolate.

And the smells! Nothing quite says Christmas like a whiff of cinnamon and vanilla from the kitchen where little drops of heaven—cookies—are baking in the oven.

Those heavenly aromas were always emanating from my Grandma Florence's kitchen. Some of my fondest memories of growing up in Wisconsin are of going to Grandma's house. No matter what time of day we stopped by, the minute the door opened my eager nose would detect a child's favorite fragrance—cookies, cakes, doughnuts, or pies—wafting through the house. Yes, she even made homemade doughnuts.

Grandma Florence was the quintessential old-time grandma: sweet, graying, plump, and always bustling about in a housedress and apron. (In my entire life, I never once saw her in pants.)

And boy, could that woman bake.

Homemade devil's food cake with boiled fluffy white frosting that cracked deliciously when you bit into it; rhubarb pie; chocolate cream pie or, my dad's favorite, lemon meringue; all kinds of cookies, including sugar, oatmeal, chocolate chip, peanut butter, spritz, and her famous fattigman bakkelse (pronounced FUT-a-mun buckles).

Fattigman is a Scandinavian (some say Danish, some say Norwegian, but Grandma was a Norwegian married to a Dane) Christmas specialty of diamond-shaped featherweight dough deep fried and rolled in powdered sugar. A holiday favorite—especially with all the men in the family. It was like biting into air—golden, delicious air with a delicate powdered sugar crunch that melted in your mouth.

Yumm.

Though not a sweet, one of my dad's holiday favorites was another Norwegian specialty—lutefisk (boiled codfish usually served with a creamed gravy or melted butter, but both Dad and Grandma preferred mustard gravy). Daddy loved the lutefisk that his mother served him every Christmas Eve.

No yumm this time.

It was a little too fishy—and blubbery—for the rest of us, so we ate Grandma's delicious Swedish meatballs and potatoes instead, always followed by julekage (YULE-a-cog), a Norwegian Christmas bread, for dessert.

I miss Grandma and her floured thumb. I inherited my sweet tooth from her.

What I didn't inherit was her year-round love of baking.

I rarely bake any other time of year (too many deadlines, too little time), yet in early December I love to break out the heavy hardware—cookie sheets—and prepare for a baking marathon.

For years my mom, my sister, and I would come together on a Saturday in early December—each bringing our favorite recipe and ingredients—and bake cookies all day long to the accompaniment of Christmas music on the stereo. Occasionally, I'd slip *White Christmas* into the VCR so we could steal glances at Bing and Rosemary making goo-goo eyes at each other while the cookies were baking. But it always seemed that whenever it got to a good part—bing! The timer would go off, and we'd have to turn back to the oven to remove the cookies before they burned.

Although once or twice I have to admit I was so caught up in what was happening on the screen that those batches came out extra crispy.

My all-time favorite Christmas cookies are the peanut butter blossoms (peanut butter cookies with Hershey's kisses planted on the top) that my Great-Aunt Lorraine from Milwaukee first introduced us to when we were little kids. It's just not Christmas without peanut butter blossoms. I especially love them warm from the oven when the chocolate kiss is still all soft and melty. Mmmm, mmmm good.

I also like to make fudge—the Kraft marshmallow kind—without nuts.

We all have our favorites.

A few years running my sister Lisa made something called "buffalo chips," which were made with oatmeal, peanut butter, chocolate chips, butterscotch chips, coconut, and something else that I can't remember now.

What I do remember is that they were mouthwateringly delicious.

Although my mom loves pecan dreams, no one else in the family likes nuts much, so instead she makes M&M

cookies and sugar cutouts for the kids and grandkids. And when my brother Todd was still alive, Grandma's fattigman bakkelse.

"One year—because they're so time-consuming—I didn't make them," Mom recalled, "and when Todd arrived, he looked at all the plates of cookies and said, 'You didn't make fattigman'?!'"

That Christmas evening, Mom and Todd spent a few happy hours making his favorite cookies together.

We're required to make cutouts at our annual baking marathon or we'd never hear the end of it from the grandkids. We used to make the sugar cookies from scratch, but lately with all the other things on our plate to bake, we've just been buying the premade slice-and-bake ones from the store, which work just as well.

Besides, it's the decorating that's the important—and fun—part.

Our cookies sport powdered sugar frosting in red, green, yellow, and blue spread atop stars and angels, snowmen and Santas, and Christmas trees and reindeer, all covered with sprinkles, colored sugars, and confetti dots. My nephew Dylan usually gets a colorful Santa with his name on it, while his sister Julia is content with a pretty pastel angel.

Michael absolutely LOVES baking at Christmastime.

He likes making lots of breads—banana, pumpkin, and zucchini—and mini carrot cake loaves to give away as gifts.

Michael makes the world's best carrot cake—incredibly moist, with no nuts, and with a secret ingredient in the cream cheese frosting—which everyone eagerly looks forward to each December. He's been asked to cater parties on the strength of his carrot cake alone. For years, however, he couldn't even sample the sweet fruits of his labor.

When we first got married, I learned that Michael had an allergic reaction to anything with cane sugar in it, which made Christmas baking kind of tricky.

But, happily, I discovered something delicious I could make that he loved—miniature fruit tarts. I'd make or buy pie dough and roll it out, then cut it into small juice glass–sized circles—making a smaller dime-sized circle in every other one. I'd fill the "bottom" circle with fresh fruit preserves—no sugar—then place the circle of dough with the small hole atop the preserves. Then, using my fancy Pampered Chef crimp-and-seal gizmo, I'd seal the top and bottom, give it a fluted edge, then bake.

Surprisingly, a couple years ago Michael's sugar allergy cleared up, and now he can eat any kind of cookie he wants. The first Christmas we realized this, I was all set to make his sugar-free fruit tarts as normal, when he said, "Forget it! I want Toll House!"

Now every year he bakes his chocolate chip cookie bars.

His sister also likes to make chocolate chip bars—but Sheri adds peanut butter to hers. Her annual holiday bake-a-thon includes three family favorites: peanut butter–chocolate chip bars, fudge—some with nuts, some without—and her husband's Christmas dessert of choice, Mexican wedding cookies.

While Sheri bakes, she likes to keep a big pot of vegetable beef soup simmering on the stove, so that at the end of the day, she and her family can relax with a nice bowl of hearty soup and bread as a nutritious alternative to all the sweets.

Food traditions are a happy and integral part of the holiday.

Pat gets together every year with her best friend Gail for their cookie-baking marathon. English toffee, Scottish shortbread, Swedish snowballs, coconut bars, and banana bread are just a few of the goodies on their must-make list.

Deciding to follow suit, one Christmas season during my single days, Lana and I, along with Janna, Andrea, and Michelle, a few girlfriends from church, decided to get in the holiday spirit with a cookie baking night. We converged on Janna's apartment, each bringing ingredients for the cookies we planned to make.

While we baked and chatted, we decided it would be fun to watch an old movie at the same time, so we put in *The Bells of St. Mary's*.

Pretty soon we were enraptured by the small screen, especially a scene where some children from the parish school rehearsed a Christmas pageant. The adorable little city boy playing Joseph was a scream. At one point, this five- or six-year-old boy took the pretty little girl playing Mary—who was a good four inches taller than him—by the hand and guided her over to the sawhorses serving as the donkey, where he hoisted her up, grunting as he did.

That's when the laughter began.

It grew as he delivered each of his unique (and we think, unscripted) lines with a special panache. When he finally learned that he and Mary could stay in the stable, after being initially rejected, he slapped his little thigh in delight and said, "Well, glory be!"

We were all laughing so hard we started crying.

And forgot what ingredients we'd already put into the cookie mixture.

Andrea and Michelle were making sugar cookies and mistakenly substituted salt for sugar—either that, or we were crying a lot more than we realized—and when the cookies came out of the oven they were inedible. Actually, they were the worst cookies ever.

Even Janna's cat wouldn't eat them. So we tossed them out and one of the girls ran to the store for some slice-and-bake cookies instead.

Whatever works. Well, glory be!

Okay, I'm getting really hungry writing this chapter, so I think it's time to stop now and do a little early holiday baking. Maybe some chocolate chip cookies, or better yet, peanut butter blossoms.

But definitely no fruitcake.

Instead of a tip at the end of this chapter, I thought you might enjoy a couple recipes instead. This first one is taken from my grandma's seventy-something-year-old handwritten recipe notebook—exactly as written. Enjoy!

Grandma Florence's Fattigman Bakkelse Recipe

1 dozen eggs (9 yolks and 3 whole eggs)
12 Tbsp. sugar
12 Tbsp. whipped cream
¾ tsp. cardamom
About 4 cups flour (not too much)
1 tsp. lemon juice
2 Tbsp. brandy
1 lump of butter the size of a walnut
Pinch of salt

Mix and cream well together (all ingredients
except flour) and keep the dough cold to be
easily handled. Then add enough flour (a little
at a time) to make a soft dough—about 4 cups.
Be sure not too much flour. Roll out very thin
and cut into diamond shapes. Cut a slit near one
end and pull other end through. Deep fry at 370
degrees. Don't fry too hard or keep the grease
too hot. Just golden color. Drain on paper
towels or brown paper. Then roll in powdered
sugar. Remember, not too much flour!

Michael's Famous Carrot Cake

2 cups sugar
3 cups flour
2 tsp. baking powder
2 tsp. baking soda
2 tsp. cinnamon

1 tsp. salt
1⅓ cup applesauce
4 eggs
2 cups shredded carrots
1 cup crushed pineapple with syrup
1 Tbsp. vanilla (yes, tablespoon)
1 tsp. orange extract

Sift together all dry ingredients—sugar, flour,
etc. (Does anybody really ever sift anymore?
We sure don't). Then add the rest of the
ingredients and mix till moistened. Beat 2
minutes at medium speed. Pour into either a
9x13 cake pan or several small greased and
floured loaf pans (if you're planning to give away
as gifts, use the disposable aluminum ones and
give it away in the pan.) Bake at 350 degrees
for 35 minutes. Let cool before frosting.

Cream Cheese Frosting

6 ounces of cream cheese (2 3-oz. packages)
4 tsp. vanilla
2 Tbsp. butter
1 tsp. almond extract ("secret" ingredient!)

Mix above ingredients till light. Then slowly add in 1 box (4 cups) powdered sugar. Frost cooled carrot cakes and enjoy!

Hint: When we give these as gifts, we usually wrap cellophane around the mini loaf, tie it with a pretty ribbon, and attach a homemade Christmas ornament to it.

6

Finding the meaning behind well-known icons of Christmas.

You'll Go Down in His Story

History is only a confused heap of facts.

Earl of Chesterfield

Laura and I are trivia buffs. It's one of the things that drew us together in our early dating days.

My fascination with useless tidbits of information is so strong that I have a standing lunch-hour appointment to play Trivial Pursuit with friends at work. Almost every week since September 1996, we've met for the challenge. (Hey, Doug and Jerry—Tuesday, noon, see ya.)

So the merging of trivia and Christmas was a natural combination.

While I have acquired lots of information, it wasn't until preparing for this chapter that I did any significant "research." Much of the findings were surprising.

Like, did you know that "The Christmas Song" was written during a heat wave in July? The story goes that two Hollywood songwriters were getting together to work on some music for a film. Because of the heat, lyricist Robert Wells was trying to cool down by making a list of "winter" things. Then Mel Torme noticed the list and in just forty minutes a song was born. "Chestnuts roasting on an open fire . . ."

Another Hollywood tidbit is that the song "White Christmas" is not originally from the film *White Christmas*. Over a decade earlier, Irving Berlin wrote the song for a Bing Crosby/Fred Astaire musical called *Holiday Inn*. Apparently, the songwriter didn't care for the song at first and was going to scrap it until Bing convinced him to keep it in the show. It won the Academy Award in 1942 and is now the best-selling Christmas song of all time.

And I'll bet you didn't know that "Jingle Bells" was really written for Thanksgiving, not Christmas, did you? Commissioned for a Medford, Massachusetts, Thanksgiving church service, it was so well received that the choir did an encore for the Christmas service. And so the song is associated with the December holiday.

There's tons of information out there about Christmas. Sure, some of it is trivial, but it seems like the history

Merry Xmas

As a kid in Sunday school, I learned we weren't supposed to use the term "X-mas" because it was an attempt to remove Christ from Christmas.

This was not the original intention. In Greek, the word Christ is Xristos, which starts with the Greek letter chi. It is our culture that changed the meaning of X to be negative.

Don't believe me? Look at the fish symbol on the backs of cars. The letters IXΘΥΣ spell the Greek word for "fish," and the letters are an acronym for the phrase "Jesus Christ, God's Son, Savior." X has been the abbreviation for "Christ" for centuries. No disrespect intended.

of the holiday and its traditions just naturally takes on more weight because it is, after all, His Story.

Have you ever stopped to think why we hack down trees and bring them inside our houses to drop needles all over the place? Or hang stockings up by the fireplace when we have dryers? Or kiss somebody just because they're standing under mistletoe? It's a parasitic plant, for goodness sake!

And then there's the big guy in the red suit. He probably has more aliases than any of the FBI's ten most wanted. What's up with that?

Does this all relate SOMEHOW to the baby in the manger?

Sure it does. Most of it, anyway. But just to warn you, some of our beliefs are not quite historical truth.

Like Jesus' birthday.

Historians agree that December 25 is not the day Jesus was born. Most likely it was in the springtime, when shepherds would be abiding (living) in the fields keeping watch over their flocks by night.

It wasn't until the early fourth century that December 25 was officially declared the Feast of the Nativity. Though the birth of Jesus was celebrated by Christians on different days in different places, this unified most everyone to the same day—and shifted some focus from pagan revelry.

The winter solstice had for centuries been a time of great celebration for many cultures throughout the world. Occurring on December 21 or 22, depending on the year, it's the shortest day and longest night of the year. In Roman times, Saturnalia was a huge festival to their god Saturn and was held during the solstice.

Since people were going to celebrate anyway, the church leaders picked that time for their sacred holiday.

Similarly, many churches today host harvest festivals on October 31 as an alternative to the pagan Halloween activities.

Criticism that Christmas has strayed from the pure and "true meaning" has been around from the beginning. From the early days it was said that there was too much of the old Saturnalia traditions blended into the Feast of the Nativity. And so it went through the centuries as different peoples blended their cultural and Christian traditions.

In the sixteenth century, the Puritans in England even set about to outlaw all festivals, including Christmas. They succeeded during the era of the Commonwealth—the mid-1600s—the period when Parliament was established and ruled in place of the kings and queens.

This same zeal against Christmas was brought by the Pilgrims to America. In fact, it was illegal to celebrate Christmas in parts of New England until just before the Civil War. Of course, many people ignored these laws. Though not able to have public celebrations, they continued to enjoy the festivities in the privacy of their homes.

As people from different cultures moved to the New World, they brought along their traditions. Melting pot that America is, we incorporated these traditions, and Christmas evolved.

At this point I'd like to make a disclaimer. I am not pretending to give a thorough history of Christmas. I've tried to hit a few highlights of those things I found personally interesting. Of course, it's subjective. Truly, I apologize to all whose customs and traditions I have omitted. There is a plethora of information available on the Internet. Try plugging "history of Christmas" into any search engine.

So here are the histories of some of our holiday icons.

The Christmas tree originated in Germany. The triangular fir tree was meant to symbolize the Holy Trinity.

Martin Luther, the Protestant Reformer, is credited for first putting candles on trees in the sixteenth century.

Trees were popularized in England—and the United States—by Queen Victoria and Prince Albert. He, being German, brought trees into their home for the royal family to enjoy.

Christmas carols date back centuries, but Saint Francis of Assisi first incorporated them into church services in the thirteenth century. Until then, the hymns in services were somber songs, usually sung in Latin. Lively folk songs were enjoyed by the public, but not in church.

Saint Francis was also the one who popularized the crèche, or Nativity scene. Christmas—and animal—lover that he was, he had a live Bethlehem scene re-enacted for his followers to explain the birth of Jesus. It caught on, both in the form of the live scene and the miniature figurines enjoyed ever since.

Although in America today our Nativity scenes usually consist of a dozen or so figures, in some cultures they bring in the whole town of Bethlehem. Some scenes include hundreds of figures, not counting all the buildings and other scenery. Sound familiar? It reminds me of the Dickens Villages so popular today.

Digressing back to Christmas carols . . .

Probably my favorite carol story is the story of "O Holy Night." Okay, I'll admit that I've loved the song ever since I heard it played solo on the piano by my second grade teacher.

To this day, I think it's the most beautiful carol ever written.

In his book *Stories behind the Best-Loved Songs of Christmas*, Ace Collins tells it so well. Placide Cappeau, a French layman and poet, was asked in 1847 to write a poem for the Christmas mass; thus was born "Cantique de Noel." His friend Adolphe Charles Adams was already a famous Parisian composer—he's best known for writing the classical ballet *Giselle*. Though he was of Jewish ancestry, Adams agreed to set "Cantique" to music and wrote it for a high solo voice with simple piano accompaniment.

"Cantique de Noel" was at first very well received. But years later, Cappeau abandoned his religion and became part of the Socialist movement. And the song was condemned by the church because it was written by a Socialist and a Jew.

About a decade later, American music critic and minister John Sullivan Dwight translated it into English. A fervent abolitionist, Dwight was moved by the lines "Chains shall He break for the slave is our brother / And in His Name all oppression shall cease." Thus, "O Holy Night" became a favorite in the United States—well, at least in the North—during the Civil War.

To quote Ace Collins, "This incredible work—requested by a forgotten parish priest, written by a poet who would later split from the church, given soaring music by a Jewish composer, and brought to Americans to serve as much as a tool to spotlight the sinful nature of slavery as tell the story of the birth of a savior—has grown to become one of the most beautiful, inspired pieces of music ever created."[1]

It should also be noted that this carol has other historical significance. It was the first song played on the radio. On Christmas Eve 1906, the first broadcast ever, the Christmas story from the Gospel of Luke was read on the air, followed by "O Holy Night" played on the violin.

Other carol stories are a mix of fact and fiction.

The story behind "Silent Night" is pretty common knowledge. The organ broke in a small Austrian town's church one Christmas Eve, so the frantic priest brought the local schoolteacher a poem he'd written and asked him to set it to music. Hours later, to guitar accompaniment, "Silent Night" made its debut. What is not common knowledge is that the poem was written two years earlier, not on the day of the service.

"God Rest Ye Merry Gentlemen" takes on a different meaning when you take into account the evolution of the English language and some missing punctuation. There used to be a comma in there. Though we sing the original words, their meaning has changed over the years. A proper translation in today's language would be something like "God make you mighty, gentlemen."

So remember that the next time you wish someone a "*Merry* Christmas."

And then there's "The Twelve Days of Christmas." Perhaps the biggest Internet urban legend of our time.

If you've had e-mail for more than a couple of years, undoubtedly you've received the one about "The Twelve Days" being a secret catechism of the Catholics in England during the 1500s. The story goes that the song was a memory aid during an era when it was too dangerous to write things down.

Unfortunately, it's not true. The catechism story only goes back as far as 1995 when an article was published—and later withdrawn. The earliest records of the song being sung in England are from the eighteenth century, not the sixteenth.

I personally like the myth and its intrigue. And the story HAS helped me remember the song. Twelve are the points in the Apostles' Creed, so it's the drummers drumming. There were eleven faithful apostles, so they're the pipers piping.

Also, the twelve days of Christmas are not the days leading up to December 25. Actually, Christmas is day one, leading up to January 6, known as the Epiphany, when it's believed the Magi arrived to visit the Christ child. While traditionally we may know the Magi as Caspar, Melchior, and Balthazar, historically, we don't even know there were three of them. It was interpreted that there were three because of the gifts—gold, frankincense, and myrrh. But the Bible only says there were Wise Men from the East. Could have been three; could have been dozens.

Other traditions tie mistletoe with Christmas. It was a solstice thing in pre-Christian England, replaced by the church in favor of the holly and the ivy as evergreen decoration. Mistletoe was popular in Victorian times and is still associated with the season.

Which brings us to our next topic—Santa Claus.

Today's Santa is an amalgam, like much of the culture in America. As people immigrated to the United

States from different countries, they brought along their holiday traditions. Present in many of these cultures is a supernatural gift giver.

Though often male, sometimes the giver is female. Like Italy's La Befana, the repentant witch who misdirected the Magi. Now she gives gifts to all children in atonement for delaying the Wise Men's search for the Christ child.

Other female gift givers are Russia's Babouschka, a grandmotherly old lady, and the German Kristkind, an angelic, fair-haired girl who wears the crown of candles. From this we get the name Kris Kringle.

In Spain and many Latin American cultures, it's the three Wise Men themselves who bring gifts.

In England he's known as Father Christmas, in France as Père Noël.

But the gift giver we know today in the United States has as his basis a bishop who lived from around A.D. 280 to 350 in Asia Minor—present day Turkey. Imprisoned for his faith by the emperor Diocletian, he was released several years later when the Christian Constantine the Great was in power.

Nicholas, bishop of Myra, became Saint Nicholas, patron saint of children. In one of the most famous stories about him, a poor man was going to have to sell his three daughters into slavery because he had no dowry to offer for them.

Anonymously, at night, on three separate occasions, bags of money arrived at their home for each of the girls, and they were able to be married. (One version of the story has the money bag thrown down the chimney and

60

landing in a stocking. This, at least in part, is where the tradition of the Christmas stockings began.) It was, of course, Nicholas who brought the gifts.

Throughout the centuries, Saint Nicholas has continued to be the favorite in Holland. His name in Dutch is Sinter Klaas, which evolved into our Santa Claus.

Much of the personality of our Santa comes from the 1822 poem by Clement Moore, known these days by its first line, "'Twas the night before Christmas." A few decades later, a political cartoonist, Thomas Nast, published his drawings of Moore's version of Santa Claus.

But it was a Depression-era advertising campaign that gave us the image of Santa that we know and love today. That company was Coca-Cola. Ever notice that Santa's clothing and the Coke label are the same color red? That was intentional.

I wonder if the people who say that Christmas has become too commercial are aware that Santa was designed to push a product? It does lend certain credibility to the argument.

But I don't care. The old Coke ads are wonderful. Some of the best ads ever created.

Which leads us to Rudolph.

He too was originally a marketing gimmick, created in 1939 for Montgomery Ward department stores. Commissioned to be a booklet given away to shoppers, the story was based in part on the tale of the ugly duckling. It has grown to become a staple in our Christmas treasury.

There are so many more things to share, and so many details I wanted to add, but Laura says this chapter is getting too long. So I'd better wrap it up.

The traditions of Christmas are many and rich. Hopefully, you've gained more from this chapter than just tidbits of knowledge for use in Trivial Pursuit—though that's not a bad thing. Some traditions are spiritual in origin, some humanitarian, and some economic. But if they add to your celebration, so much the better. Merry Christmas.

Historical Tips

This year, why not share with others the histories of the icons of Christmas? I told you about some of them here. But what other icons do you include in your celebration of Christmas? How about doing a little research of your own and finding out their origins? Like why do we eat turkey at Christmas? What, exactly, is the story behind the Advent candle? And why is it that we mail billions of Christmas cards each year? Knowing the "whys" just might help you enjoy them all the more.

7

Holiday collections can make the season bright.

collectible christmas

By wisdom a house is built,
and through understanding it is
established;
through knowledge its rooms are filled
with rare and beautiful treasures.

Proverbs 24:3–4

I n the mid-1980s, while shopping at the mall, I (Michael) came across two small ceramic figurines of Father Christmas. Definitely European and probably nineteenth century in design. Different than all the Santa Clauses I was used to seeing, these were old-world and had that certain something that said they belonged in my apartment.

The following summer I was on tour with the theater troupe I belonged to, and July found us in Colorado Springs. It was probably the first time I'd noticed a Christmas shop open all year, so I decided to investigate.

And there it was.

A music box of Santa Claus kneeling before the Christ Child in the manger, Santa's cap respectfully removed and lying on the floor, his hands folded in prayer. More than intrigued, I picked it up and wound the spring. When it played "O Come Let Us Adore Him," it all clicked. Santa Claus. Saint Nicholas. Of course a saint would worship Jesus. His adoration for the Holy One would motivate all his other actions. Though I could ill afford it on my actor's salary, I bought the music box.

Now I had an official collection.

That year I think I bought two or three more figures and decided that too much of a good thing was still too much. So I decided to limit myself to only one Father Christmas per year.

But that didn't stop family and friends from adding to my collection. Except for the music box, almost all my Father Christmases are old-fashioned, old-world looking. This many years later, I still hold to my tradition of buying only one for myself per year, though Laura also buys me one a year now, too. We have fun searching for months for just the right figure, being careful to not buy it too soon, because we might find a better one later.

At this point, I think I should mention that there has been a year or two when another Father Christmas made it into the house—"purchased" for me by our dog, Gracie.

Isn't Collecting Expensive?

That depends on your collection. Eighteenth-century original oil paintings would be expensive. Even the Dickens Village collectibles can be considered pricey.

But almost all of my Father Christmas figures were inexpensive—at least the ones Laura and I have purchased—most under fifteen dollars, and many less than ten. Of course, there are a few exceptions, and I cannot provide an accounting for the ones given by friends and family.

Much of the fun is in the hunt, looking for the bargains. And that's what this collection is all about. Many collections are "investments"; this one's for fun.

My collection is now pushing sixty figures. Okay, maybe dragging sixty. Yet each one is special and has the year and other significant information written on the bottom or back.

Cost, of course, has little to do with the value I place on my Father Christmases. The one made from printed fabric, filled with polyester stuffing, and dated 1992 is one of my most valuable. Purchased for a couple of dollars at a craft fair on Apple Hill, it represents a "good day" during Laura's chemotherapy.

A figure of a nautically dressed Santa with a life preserver around his middle was sent to me by my mom when I was working on the cruise ship. No subtlety there—only a mother could be so concerned about her son being that far from land. Okay, I know it's not a Father Christmas, but it was too perfect for the circumstances.

And the one I keep out all year, from our friends Pat and Ken, of the old man in brown knickers and a green plaid wool shirt. He's sitting on a bench, adding the heart to a toy teddy bear. During the holidays, he's Father Christmas. The rest of the time, he's just Grandpa.

In September 2001, Laura and I took our long-awaited vacation to England. The ancient city of York—a walled city where you can still walk around atop its walls—was one of our favorite places. Constantine was crowned emperor of the Roman Empire there in A.D. 436, and the York Minster is one of the greatest Gothic cathedrals in the world—beautiful and majestic. We were thrilled to be able to attend Evensong services there.

Our first day in York, we decided to split up—Laura needed to check e-mail at the Internet café, I wanted to do some touristy things—and meet up later for tea-time.

Glancing through the tourist information brochure, I spotted an ad for the Christmas Angels shop—open all year. Aha! I might find this year's Father Christmas in his homeland—England. I looked through the store, not seeing one until I got to the back corner. Late 1800s–looking with two Victorian children on a sled. Practically the most wonderful figure I'd ever seen.

66

With an equally wonderful price tag. "Dear," as the Brits would say. Well, I had to check with Laura before spending that much, so I headed over to the Internet café.

Laura was excited when she saw me. She hadn't gone directly to the café but had hit a gift store across from the Minster and found the Father Christmas she would give me that year.

"Here, open it," she beamed.

I opened the bag and then the box. It was beautiful. And very different from any other in my collection. It was a profile, in mid-stride, with a pale blue cloak. But his hat was broken.

When we exchanged it, I saw what a bargain it was. Which, of course, escalated the extravagance of the one I had found. But still hoping, I invited Laura to go check out Christmas Angels. We made our way to the shop, then to the back corner. When she saw the Father Christmas, she immediately agreed that it was wonderful and was the one I should buy that year.

Then she saw the price.

"Well, it's English as English can be," she said.

"And it's from York," I added.

"It's fabulous."

"Isn't it?"

Pause.

"It needs to be in your collection."

Score.

When we saw the box, we realized there was no way we could fit it into our luggage, so we decided to ship it home. The clerk didn't know the exact shipping cost and, since it was late on a Sunday afternoon, couldn't call anyone to find out, but we made the arrangements anyway.

When we got our Visa bill, we discovered that the shipping was more than the purchase price.

Are we sorry we bought it? No way.

Sorry we didn't make room in the luggage? You betcha.

While the Father Christmas from York turned out to be the most expensive of any in my collection—and has phenomenal memories to go along with it as well—it's no match in sentimental value for the trio my mother made for me.

One late November afternoon during our first year of marriage, Laura and I were unpacking some boxes of decorations I'd had in storage. I opened one marked "fragile" and carefully pulled out the large figures.

"These were powder when Mom started making them," I explained. "She mixed and poured the slip (liquid clay) and fired them in her own kiln."

I showed Laura the one with the sapphire-blue, flowing coat and the biggest one with the reindeer. I pointed out to her my mom's attention to detail, especially the eyes. "The mark of true artistry and craftsmanship is in the eyes," I said.

Then I pulled out the dark green figure. The lines were not as crisp and the eyes were fuzzy—obviously painted by a shaky hand.

"That's when Mom was sick."

Mom had been ill for years. In fact, the doctors had given her "weeks, maybe months," to live, and that was almost four years earlier.

It was a nice afternoon, reminiscing with my bride about my mom and family and our holidays past. Then we went over to dinner at a friend's house.

When we got home, we learned that my mom had passed away that evening.

I will always be grateful that at the end of my mom's life on earth, I was sharing wonderful memories of her.

Thanks to my collection.

Collectible Tip

You don't have to go overboard to be a collector. (I know, I know. I'm talking to myself here also.) Nor do you have to spend a lot of money. You just have to LOVE whatever it is you collect.

Even if it's only a collection of one.

From It's a Wonderful Life to Ralphie and his Red Ryder BB gun, snuggling in with favorite Christmas movies.

8

Zuzu's Petals

God gave us memory that we might have roses in December.

J. M. Barrie

"*Z*uzu's petals!"

If those two little words are Greek to you, then you're not a dyed-in-the-wool fan of the best-loved Christmas movie of all time, *It's a Wonderful Life.* If you've never seen this Jimmy Stewart holiday classic, run, don't walk, to the nearest video store and rent it this minute! (And watch very carefully toward the end of the film for that famous line.)

Michael and I love that movie. But then, we love a *lot* of Christmas movies. In fact, when we got married, we were delighted to discover that we both love to sing along with Bing, bake Christmas cookies, and watch the same Christmas movies year after year: *White Christmas, Miracle on 34th Street, It's a Wonderful Life, A Christmas Story,* and, of course, *A Charlie Brown Christmas.*

We also love *Rudolph the Red-Nosed Reindeer,* which many people like to watch with their children. But since we don't have kids, we simply wholeheartedly embrace the child within us and enjoy it just as much. Every year, we recite favorite lines to each other: "She thinks I'm cu-u-u-te!" "*I* want to be a dentist," and "It's not beawwy compfuble," work really well at home as we gaze lovingly into each other's eyes, but as witty office repartee, we get a few blank looks.

I especially love it when the doe Clarice sings "There's Always Tomorrow" to the disconsolate Rudolph, who's been kicked out of the reindeer games thanks to his shiny red nose. I bat my doe eyes at Michael and sing along about "believ[ing] in your dreams come what may."

I always love a good romantic song.

And speaking of romance—and the holidays—*It's a Wonderful Life* has one of the most romantic love scenes ever captured on film.

Don't believe me?

Fast forward your videotape or DVD until you get to the part where George (Jimmy Stewart) has dropped by Mary's (Donna Reed's) house to visit. Their conversation hasn't gone well, and he starts to leave in anger just as the phone rings and Mary answers a call from their old school chum Sam—Hee-Haw—Wainwright, now a rich businessman. As George returns to retrieve his forgotten hat, Sam tells Mary to put George on the phone too.

With their heads bent close together next to the shared phone receiver, you can see the romantic tension build and build as George, the dreamer who has longed for adventure his whole life, tries to fight his feelings for the sweet hometown girl who has loved him ever since the second grade.

George loses the fight. And his heart. And that scene makes my heart go pitty-pat every time.

Trust me. And if you don't want to trust me, then trust the American Film Institute, who listed it among their top ten U.S. screen romances of all time. (It came in at No. 8, behind such passionate favorites as *Casablanca, Gone with the Wind, An Affair to Remember,* and *Doctor Zhivago.*)

We're not the only ones who love *It's a Wonderful Life.*

One holiday season Michael decided to spice up his department's dry monthly newsletter at work, so he put on his roving reporter hat and traveled far and wide— okay, he stood by the Pepsi machine at lunchtime—to ask his coworkers what their favorite Christmas movie was.

Naturally, *It's a Wonderful Life* came in first, followed by *Miracle on 34th Street,* while close on its heels was *A Christmas Story*—with Ralphie and his Red Ryder BB gun. Next came Bing Crosby and the gang in *White Christmas,* and fifth place was a tie between *Rudolph the Red-Nosed Reindeer* and the original *How the Grinch Stole Christmas.*

Those are my top five, too.

Even *The Sound of Music* received a couple of votes. (Do *you* remember Maria and the Captain around a Christmas tree? Me neither, but I do love this movie and seem to recall it often plays on TV during the holidays . . .)

White Christmas is like an old, comfortable sweater we pull out every year when the weather turns cold. Great songs sung by the wonderful Rosemary Clooney and Bing Crosby, fabulous dancing by Danny Kaye and Vera Ellen, gorgeous costumes, all set in the nostalgic days just after World War II.

Michael and I agree that "The Best Things Happen When You're Dancing" is one of our favorite musical dance numbers in all the movies. When I was young, I'd pretend to be the graceful Vera Ellen with the teeny-tiny waist, dancing around the living room.

But since I was never graceful, nor did I have a teeny-tiny waist, I decided to leave the dancing to her. I did like the "Sisters" duet so much, though, that I performed it in the ninth-grade talent show with my best friend Cheryl Kaiser. (Once I also made my baby brother Timmy—whom I christened Timothea for the occasion—don a dress and one of my mom's old wigs and sing it with me for the family. He hasn't forgotten, or forgiven me, to this very day.)

What can I say? It was a big sister thing.

But mostly, whenever I watch this familiar favorite, I think of my dad—especially the part near the end

where Bing and Danny lead the military chorus in singing to their forgotten general, "We'll follow the old man
wherever he wants to go . . ."

That part makes me tear up every time without fail.

A Christmas Story, on the other hand, makes me fall
on the floor laughing without fail—every single time.

Filmed in 1981 but set in the 1940s, and based on
humorist Jean Shepherd's *In God We Trust, All Others
Pay Cash* memoir, it's the hysterical tale of a little boy
named Ralphie who desperately wants a Red Ryder
BB gun for Christmas. (Or as Ralphie would say, "an
official Red Ryder carbine action two hundred shot
range model air rifle with a compass in the stock and
this thing that tells time.")

But his mother, teacher, and almost every other
grown-up in the film—including the department store
Santa—are dead set against the idea, warning him,
"You'll shoot your eye out!"

This more recent classic is one of the most scream-
ingly funny movies ever made—definitely the funniest
Christmas movie of all time. And so beloved and familiar to us, we simply call it "Ralphie." Michael's sister
Sheri, her husband, Jim, and their family are so in love
with this perennial favorite that it kicks off their Christmas season every year—on Thanksgiving night.

After a full day of turkey, mashed potatoes and gravy,
and all the trimmings, they relax and enjoy a little Ralphie with their pumpkin pie. Michael and I have had the
pleasure of joining them a few times for this much-loved
holiday tradition. We all sit around and recite favorite
lines together. This one is our favorite: "Randy lay there

Don't Forget the Books!

While most of the great Christmas stories have been made into films that we love, we also have our favorites on the printed page. For those of you fellow bibliophiles, we enjoy reading—and displaying—the following books each Christmas:

A Christmas Carol, Charles Dickens
A Child's Christmas in Wales, Dylan Thomas
Christmas Every Day, William Dean Howells
Let's Keep Christmas, Peter Marshall
A Charlie Brown Christmas, Charles Schulz
How the Grinch Stole Christmas, Dr. Seuss
Rudolph the Red-Nosed Reindeer (reproduction of the original), Robert L. May
The Best Christmas Pageant Ever, Barbara Robinson
When Mother Was Eleven-Foot-Four, Jerry Camery Hoggatt

like a slug. It was his only defense." I'm telling you, you've GOTTA see this movie!

Part of *A Christmas Story* was filmed in Cleveland, Ohio, where I was living at the time. It's fun to see the Higbee's window scene at the beginning because I shopped at Higbee's and even had a friend who worked there.

A well-known New York storefront plays a prominent role in another of our most-loved Christmas movies,

Miracle on 34th Street. Michael and I were delighted a couple years ago when we visited the Big Apple for the first time together and got to walk by Macy's on the corner of 34th Street.

Both of us grew up with this delightful black-and-white Maureen O'Hara–Natalie Wood classic, and it will forever hold a nostalgic place in our hearts. My favorite part comes near the end of the movie when little Susan (Natalie) doesn't get the Christmas present she asked for—a house in the country. She's sitting in the car woodenly repeating the refrain, "I believe. I believe. It's silly, but I believe," when suddenly she screams out to her mom (Maureen O'Hara) and her mom's love interest (John Payne), who's driving, "Stop the car!"

Susan bolts out of the car and races up the steps to the little house she's always dreamed of—with a swing in the backyard—which she asked Santa for, and which just happens to be for sale.

Don't you just love sappy happy endings? I do—especially at Christmastime.

Speaking of that, I can't believe I nearly forgot one of the greatest Christmas classics of all time: *A Christmas Carol.* There have been numerous remakes of this wonderful Dickens story filmed over the years—including a humorous take called *Scrooged* with Bill Murray—but the best of the bunch, in my opinion, is the 1951 Alastair Sim version. Michael's personal favorite, however, is *An American Christmas Carol* with Henry Winkler—the Fonz.

If you're not moved by Tiny Tim and this wondrously uplifting story of transformation—in any of the renditions —then it's time to hand in your Christmas stocking.

Still not in the holiday mood? Feeling a little bah humbug, perhaps? Maybe you're echoing a line from another great classic: "I think there must be something wrong with me, Linus. Christmas is coming, but I'm not happy."

Well, you Charlie Brown, it's time to hit your local video store and rent any—or all—of the Christmas movies we've mentioned. Before you know it, you'll be humming, "Have a holly, jolly Christmas. It's the best time of the year." (Can you name *that* movie?)

Movie Tip

Try watching Christmas movies in July to cool off.
Michael's Grandma Adelaide, who often baby-sat her great-grandkids when they were growing up, would pop in Christmas videos filled with snow and ice in July and August to help them forget the scorching Sacramento days of summer. (For even more fun, do what we do and host a Christmas-in-July party with your friends and have a marathon movie day!)

Of nutcrackers, Messiah sing-alongs, and neighborhoods lit up like the Electric Light Parade.

9

Those Not-So-Silent Nights

You need three things in the theatre—the play, the actors, and the audience, and each must give something.

Kenneth Haigh

Laura and I both feel the season is hardly complete without some kind of live performance.

Last year, we joined my sister and her family for the *Nutcracker Ballet.* Laura and I usually like to sit in the balcony for shows with a lot of dancing—that way we get a great view of the whole stage and the "big picture." At Sheri's suggestion, however, this time we sat close. We're talking third row from the stage. A great place to see all the dancers' expressions and the details of the sets and costumes. Sitting so close, we noticed other things, too—one young male dancer was having a bit of trouble with the lifts. We could even see the strain on his face as he hoisted the ballerina over his head again and again.

After the performance, as we were walking back to the car, my sister remarked, "Bless his heart, he's just not built big enough for all those moves."

Had we been in the balcony, or even in the middle of the auditorium, I'm sure we would not have noticed.

December is also a big month for professional and community theaters. Over the years we've seen a few different productions of Dickens's *A Christmas Carol* along with numerous original holiday programs.

And then there are the church productions. Sheri and her family attend a large church that always has something going on at Christmas. There was the year we went to see the musical in which my niece, her then seventeen-year-old daughter Jennie, portrayed Mary and sang her first solo—the Amy Grant song "Breath of Heaven."

It was perfect.

Though Jennie has had no formal vocal training, she nailed it. There were others besides me—her proud and admittedly biased uncle (who *has* had vocal train-ing)—who thought she sang it better than Amy Grant. Jennie WAS Mary, a teenaged woman who was still a girl, nervous because she was in unfamiliar territory, so totally outside of anything she'd ever experienced.

Singing alone for the first time in front of hundreds of people, Jennie too was in unfamiliar territory. Her nervousness added to the performance and allowed us to experience how Mary might have felt in Bethlehem, giving birth to the Son of God.

I wept through the entire song and still tear up, this many years later, at the memory.

It's one of my favorite memories of a Christmas cantata—including all the ones in which I performed.

Laura has performed at Christmastime too—while she was stationed overseas in the Air Force in England. In a traditional English pantomime, no less.

"Traditional" English pantomime is usually a much-loved children's story performed during the holidays with a woman playing the principal boy character (think Mary Martin or Cathy Rigby as Peter Pan).

I'll let her tell the story from here. Take it away, honey.

While living in Oxfordshire, England, I (Laura) was the only American in the theater company of a small village near the base. So I was surprised and delighted when I learned I'd won the lead role of Aladdin for the Christmas pantomime.

Although it felt a little strange at first to be playing a boy, I did so in a thigh-length Mandarin jacket (I was thinner then), black tights, high heels, and lots of stage makeup. I threw myself into the role with gusto, even trying to look appropriately smitten when I had to sing a love song to the princess.

Everything was going great until I said the line, "Uncle, where's the lamp?"

Keep in mind that I'm originally from Wisconsin and still bear the traces of that nasal Midwestern accent. Having lived in England for a couple years, however, I'd picked up a bit of an English accent and had easily gotten into the habit of saying things like "Ack-shualy" (actually), "toe-mah-to" rather than "to-may-to," and "po-tah-to" rather than "po-tay-to." I also said things like "I'll ring you up" rather than "call you" and "would you like a bit of bread?" instead of "a piece" of bread. They were part of my daily lexicon.

But there were still a few words I couldn't say the way the English did without feeling a bit pretentious. Such as "al-loo-min-ium" for aluminum and "shed-yule" for "schedule." And . . . you guessed it, "lahmp" for lamp.

It sounded so to-the-manor-born, which I most definitely wasn't, and forced and artificial. Besides, Aladdin was a tale from the Middle East, so an English accent wasn't a requirement. Unfortunately, with my Midwestern nasal twang, when I said, "Uncle, where's the lamp?" it came out "la-a-a-a-anmp."

And got the biggest—unintended—laugh of the evening.

What can I say? You can take the girl out of Wisconsin, but apparently you can't take Wisconsin out of the girl.

Back to you now, honey.

Thanks, dear. With all the choral music we have sung and heard, Laura and I have yet to attend a Handel's *Messiah* sing-along. Sure we've sung the Hallelujah Chorus. And a few other songs from the *Messiah* have been included in other programs. Still, we've missed hearing it in its entirety.

Maybe that's because for most of our married life I'd been involved in *An Evening in December*, the pageant extravaganza our former church, First Covenant, puts on. Every year the program is different, but it still has the same name. And my involvement usually started during the summer.

It's a huge show.

The cast usually includes over two hundred performers—actors and soloists, two adult choirs, the youth choir, and the children's choir, plus a small ensemble or two. There's a play and, of course, tons of music.

Because of my theater background, I've been fortunate to participate in many aspects of the pageant, which was great for my innate need for variety. I've acted, sung in the choir and as a soloist, directed the actors, and designed what seems like millions of props.

Like the year we needed 120 hula hoops braided with red and green tinsel garland, which had to be securely fastened so the hoops could be tossed, spinning into the air. Or the three-foot-tall plywood candy canes we made for the "hat and cane" soft-shoe number. Fortunately, there were always people helping with the mass production. (Thanks again, honey, for painting all the canes white and wrapping the red electrical tape for the stripes.)

83

The very first year I was involved in *An Evening in December,* I was cast as C. J., the narrator of the show. The show was medieval in theme and set in a castle, and C. J. was the royal court jester.

We were all responsible for coming up with our own costumes. While I originally envisioned a bright red and yellow Peter Pan–like outfit for C. J., John, the writer/director/producer, had a different color scheme in mind.

"How would you feel in purple and pink?" he asked one day.

I was secretly mortified but hid it well.

"What shades would you like?" I replied in my best professional actor tone.

"Grape and fuchsia."

"You got it."

And so it was. Split down the middle, grape purple on one side and fuchsia pink on the other, with a pointy pink collar, black tights, and turtleneck.

Only problem was the shoes.

It was a very physical role. The set was three stories tall with winding staircases on either side of the stage. I was literally running up and down the stairs and across from one side to the other. I needed my athletic shoes.

So I made some Wizard of Oz munchkin–looking, curvy-toed shoe covers out of the pink fabric. It was the best I could come up with at the time. I glued Velcro to the shoes and to the covers. Once my sneakers were on and laced securely, I could strap on the facades.

Laura and others—including my mother-in-law and friends from work—said it was quite a sight to behold.

I think it had something to do with the extra fabric and the thickness of the Velcro, which made the shoes disproportionate to the rest of my body. Kind of like Bozo-the-clown shoes.

If Bozo wore pink.

But that wasn't all. When John was writing the play that year, he thought it would be funny to have a whole section done in alliteration. Everything beginning with the letter *J*. Pretty much every *J* word he could think of was crammed into one monologue for that moment in the play when everything goes wrong and the best-laid plans all backfire.

"Oh, I can't believe this is happening. I'm a jilted jester. I'll be jostled from the kingdom. I'll be the jester they use for jousting practice," was just the beginning. "I'm a joke. I'm in a jam. My world's a jumble."

And then my favorite part: "I'll be a big jest in a jump through the journey of jester journalism."[2]

Before we started rehearsals, people who read the script thought John was crazy for writing it that way. But he believed in it—and in me.

It was probably the hardest monologue I've ever memorized; I was determined to get it right. I spent weeks working on it. Even reciting it while on my daily walks at work.

It must have seemed strange to coworkers, seeing someone talking to himself, especially with all those *J* words.

I'm just glad I wasn't wearing the pink shoes at the time.

But the hard work paid off. It was definitely fun to perform. And it was a great part of the show.

That was my first of seven *An Evening in December* productions.

Last year we moved to a different church. While I was invited and encouraged to still be part of the pageant, I was not able to. Our vacation to England and then October being Breast Cancer Awareness Month—a big month for speaking engagements for us both—did not allow my involvement. But we were there in the audience on opening night.

It was great to see that I was involved after all as I spied many of the props I had made over the years.

And with that, I'll still be there for years to come.

Show Tips

Any live performance would not be complete without an audience. One director I worked with called it "the final cast member." So even if you are not a performer, you can still be part of the show. Call up a friend or two and order some tickets. Adding dinner before or dessert and tea/coffee afterward makes for a fun and memorable not-so-silent night.

Or, taking the bah out of humbug. What happens when someone in the family is a Scrooge?

10

God Rest Ye Grumpy Scroogeymen

If I could work my will, every idiot who goes about with "Merry Christmas" on his lips, should be boiled with his own pudding, and buried with a stake of holly through his heart.

Ebenezer Scrooge in Dickens's *A Christmas Carol*

Bah humbug.
Too commercial.
Too expensive.
Too exhausting.

Tom was a grown-up who didn't like Christmas. He was the Scrooge to end all Scrooges.

Until he married Lily.

Now he admits that growing up, Christmas didn't like him, so the feeling became mutual.

As the youngest of seven kids, Tom always got hand-me-downs. And his financially struggling parents had one kind of socks for the boys. Solid white and interchangeable. Just wash, dry, grab any two, and stuff 'em in a drawer. Any boy's drawer, since they were all fished from the same sock pool.

Tom ached for colored socks so he could be like the rest of the kids at school.

One year that's all he asked for at Christmas.

So his parents bought him several pairs. All mustard yellow.

Tom felt humiliated. Sure, in the grand scheme of things, why should socks be so important? He had food to eat and a place to call home, and he did have clothing, including shoes and socks.

But Christmas isn't about physical needs. It's emotional and spiritual. And this little boy's spirit was being chipped away.

This is the same kid who participated in a white-elephant gift exchange when he was in the Boy Scouts.

He got a prune.

And these are just two of the disappointments Tom experienced during his formative years. In order to get through the holidays, he just stopped caring.

Laura and I have a theory that says many people are Scrooges because of disappointment. But it doesn't have to stay that way.

When Tom married Lily, they decided to redeem Christmas for each other.

Lily loved Christmas. But it seemed like every man in every former relationship had bailed out just before the holidays.

According to the Oxford American Dictionary, *redeem* means "to buy back, to recover [a thing] by payment or by doing something." Also, "to make up for faults or deficiencies." Grown-up and newly married, Tom and Lily started new holiday traditions. Now, several years later, Christmas is a wonderful time for them both.

Tom, especially, has learned how to have fun with the season. It's called planning.

One year he restored an old illuminated clock that had been in Lily's father's barn for decades—since before Lily could remember. Now it sits atop Lily and Tom's entertainment center. While Tom had the clockworks professionally rebuilt, he rewired the lights himself. For the man who describes himself as "technologically challenged," this was no small task. He taught himself as he went along.

What a huge act of love. Which makes the clock all the more precious to Lily.

Taking the time to plan and then spending the energy to execute that plan does much to make the season bright.

Though most of her season is bright, our friend Rebecca is a little "Scrooged-off" about Christmas cards.

She wants to know how come when she got married she had to assume the job of writing all her husband's Christmas cards.

"I love my husband to death and he's generally a wonderful, enlightened man. But I was really surprised the first Christmas after we got married when he started rolling off a list of his friends and relatives that *I* needed to send cards to. And of course, he only started mentioning it a week before December 25."

His reasoning? She's the writer in the family. "Besides," he says, "women are better at it." He'll sometimes alternate that excuse with, "Your penmanship is better."

He'll sign the cards—bulk production style—to help, but it's her job to keep up the addresses and write all the messages.

"So to this day, I write all the Christmas cards, and struggle with finding clever little things to say to relatives of his I've never met, and pretend like those notes are heartfelt and sent from both of us," says Rebecca. "All this to relatives and obscure friends whom he never ever contacts (except for *my* Merry Christmas cards each year!)."

Sometimes it's not a matter of what role you are fulfilling; it's just a matter of not knowing what to do.

Like my new brother-in-law Mike. Because he'd never spent much time or energy on Christmas, he thought himself quite the Scroogeyman. Then he proposed to my sister Debbie. Little did he realize that Scrooginess doesn't stand a chance in our family. Kind

Snap Out of It!

We like to encourage people. That's why we're suckers for Girl Scouts selling cookies in front of the supermarket.

That's also why I (Michael) try to always carry change when I go into the stores at Christmas—for the bell ringers.

Be they Salvation Army volunteers or Santa impersonators, they stand there for hours while people pass them by, pretending not to see them. How discouraging.

So I give them my spare change. No skin off my nose, but it can make a difference. Last year one man seemed outright surprised that someone gave. I'll never know the real story behind that look he gave me, but I'd like to think he was encouraged that someone cared.

of like standing in front of an avalanche and saying, "I've never been much for snow."

Good luck.

Mike did okay for their first Christmas together, especially for a self-professed Ebenezer. But Debbie decided to enlighten him the next year. She took him to the mall. They had fun strolling through the shops, Debbie fawning over this and that.

Mike took the hint, and then some. My sister was surprised at some of the gifts she received.

"Peace beads," she said, wonderingly. "I got peace beads."

"Anytime I said, 'This is nice,' he bought it for me," she added. "It was very thoughtful and sweet, but just because I say, 'This is nice,' doesn't mean I want it."

This year will be their third Christmas together. We'll see what happens. But remember, Debbie, getting good at doing Christmas is a skill that takes time. And Mike only has one day a year to practice.

At least he's willing to shop.

Unlike our neighbor Al, who can't stand shopping. So he'll just give his wife, Dolores, money and let her pick out what she wants.

Laura's Uncle Jimmy is the same way. He HATES shopping. So every Christmas he puts money into envelopes for Sharon and the kids and clips them to the tree. He even does this for his grandkids.

We think they are just natural born Scrooges.

The solution? Celebrate around them. Maybe eventually they'll join in the Christmas cheer—especially if you tease them enough. Or maybe not. Some people just like being the Grinch.

Come to think of it, neither Al nor Jimmy has a dog. Maybe, just maybe, if they had a dog named Max they could put little antlers on . . .

But that's another story altogether.

Grumpy Scroogeyman Advice

If you have a grumpy Scroogeyman in your life, start singing him this song. Perhaps he'll change his tune.

God rest ye grumpy Scroogeymen,
   let no one you dismay.
Remember joy at Christmastime,
   at least on Christmas Day.
Don't be a jerk, take off from work,
   let Rudolph light your way.
And find kids to play with today,
   hear what I say.
And don't forget to be a kid today!

Christmas is a family affair, and a couple constitutes a family.

11

Just the Two of Us

For this reason a man will leave his
father and mother and be united to his
wife, and they will become one flesh.

Genesis 2:24

Baking Christmas cookies, wrapping presents to put beneath the tree, watching *Rudolph the Red-Nosed Reindeer* for the zillionth time with the kids . . . Wait a minute! What if there aren't any kids? What's Christmas like without children?

Just as special—but in different ways.

Christmas is a time for families. And a husband and wife make up their own family. But often couples without children tend to get overlooked in the whole focus-on-the-family/kids holiday.

Many couples don't have children. Some make the choice; others have the choice made for them; some are still newlyweds; some have already "been there, done that" and their children have flown the coop and are feathering their own Christmas nests. Whatever the circumstance, not having youngsters shouldn't diminish the childlike joy we have in Christmas.

Besides, what's to say that WE can't be the children?

"It's never too late to have a happy childhood," Michael often says.

That happy childhood is never more evident than at Christmastime when we deck the halls, make popcorn balls, and set up the train under the tree.

Charles Dickens, author of the much-loved *A Christmas Carol*, said, "It is good to be children sometimes, and never better than at Christmas, when its mighty Founder was a child Himself."

Amen to that.

In our family of two—now three, including our dog, Gracie—we LOVE Christmas!

We go all out for our favorite holiday. Shopping all year round—keeping our eyes peeled in secondhand bookstores and one-of-a-kind boutiques for just the right present for each person. Starting as early as February or March to make special handcrafted gifts. Even hosting a Christmas-in-July party when we get a hankering for the winter festivities during the heat of a California summer.

Before we met, Michael and I were individual Christmas nuts, but together we're a whole pile of chestnuts roasting on an open fire. Even though we don't have kids, we don't let that stop us from celebrating this most special of days that began with the most important birth in history.

Yet celebrating the birth of a baby when you can't have your own baby can be difficult.

After years of infertility treatments and disappointments, my friend Laurie just couldn't face another Christmas with step-grandchildren and extended family.

"I wanted to escape, to find a place where there were no children at Christmas," Laurie said. "Although it seemed shocking and selfish at the time, my husband and I decided to bow out of all the holiday hoopla and headed to Maui for two weeks. Some family members were sure we'd be totally homesick and regret it. Nothing remotely like that happened. Instead, we were freed from the overspending and last-minute gift buying. Freed from the endless crowds and advertisements. Freed from making my home look like something Martha [Stewart] would approve of. Freed from slaving over a hot stove in the kitchen and then cleaning up.

"Instead," she says, "I learned to surf and indulged myself in my new sport every morning. We explored the island, went snorkeling, and ate delicious meals under swaying palm trees. We saw the green flash at sunset. (If the weather is right—clear and humid—the moment the sun dips below the horizon, an unexplained bright green flash occurs.) We went to a casual outdoor Christmas Eve service where everyone wore leis and sang under the stars. It was relaxing, romantic, and more fun than we could have imagined.

"Sometimes you need to just get away to bolster yourself and your marriage," Laurie says.

Yep.

And one of these years, Michael and I plan to do exactly that—we're just waiting for Santa to stick a couple of airline tickets in our Christmas stockings. Meanwhile, we'll continue to enjoy our California Christmas with friends and relatives.

Diane, my former Air Force roommate, and her husband, Warren, who now live in Arizona, generally spend Christmas alone together since their families live in other states. They put up their tree two weeks before the holiday, and Diane plays Christmas music and has potpourri simmering throughout the house. "All the memories of Germany and England come back when I put the ornaments we got over there on the tree," she said.

The two of them also enjoy cooking Christmas dinner together.

Food—and its preparation—plays a big role in their household.

"We usually don't buy huge gifts for each other, but a lot of little gifts instead," said Diane. "I'm happy getting Earl Grey tea, honey mustard pretzels, Red Vines, and Sour Patch Kids. Just a few of my favorite things, and gee, you can eat every gift! I love to eat—it's my favorite pastime in life. I guess I've always believed in 'If I can't eat it or wear it, I don't need it.' Warren gets off pretty easy shopping for me at the grocery store."

Our friends Jan and Carl always say they're not going to do Christmas presents for each other. Instead, they'll

Blended Family Couples

If you're remarried and part of a new blended family, it's still important to do something for "just the two of you," so you might consider doing what my girlfriend did.

Every Christmas Eve she and her "new" husband don their Santa hats and load the car with goodies they've made and make unannounced visits to all their friends in town. "One year it was my apricot jam, another it was biscotti and English toffee.

"Whoever isn't home, we leave notes on the porch. Those who are home are thrilled. We don't stay long—unless begged—but it makes Christmas, a time of stress because of the fractured family, a bit more special because it's our own tradition that has nothing to do with the children."

save their money for their traveling dreams. (That couple has been to Europe more times than years they've been married. But I'm not jealous. Not at all.)

Yet for a stocking stuffer, Jan—an Anglophile, who's picked up some British expressions—will always tell Carl, "I'd rather love some songs from my favorite movies.

"I have yet to see one tape or CD," she giggles. "I think his hearing's starting to go. . . . Perhaps he thinks I say 'lather' and 'scrub' instead of 'rather love,' because I always get scented bubble bath and a fancy sponge."

Kyle and Lesley, some other friends of ours who don't have children, begin their Christmas season in early December with the church musical extravaganza.

"Excitement builds at the steps of the main entrance of the auditorium with a mandatory hug with Father Christmas," the English-born Lesley says. "Then into the show—an hour and a half of singing, clapping, and laughing, and occasionally, a tear.

"The next day welcomes in the seasonal trauma of untwisting the lights and checking the strings for duff bulbs," she says. "It's Kyle's job to hang the lights, and I busy myself with the dressing of the tree.

"When the lights are dimmed and the candles lit, it's all a little reminiscent of the disco era as the flickering light dances its way across all the sparkly hanging ornaments."

Christmas Eve kicks off Kyle and Lesley's traditional Christmas movie marathon. They turn off the phone and "shut down the hatches" so they won't be disturbed as they snuggle in with their holiday favorites. Christmas morning they exchange gifts, Lesley makes Kyle his favorite pancakes, and she calls her family in England. Then it's back to their movies, followed by lunch at one of Kyle's sisters', where the whole family gathers for gift giving.

"But Christmas night is ours," Lesley stresses. "Me, hubby, and the pooch."

Michael and I always try to reserve a portion of Christmas Day to spend time alone together—just the two of us. But with many members of both sides of our families in the same town, that's often next to impossible.

Usually, if we wake up early enough, we'll spend an hour or so in the morning exchanging our gifts. But if we "sleep in"—past eight—we forego our alone time until later in the day so that we'll make it over to breakfast at Sheri and Jim's in time for their annual family Christmas open house. Christmas dinner at my mom's is often late afternoon or early evening, but it varies from year to year.

Occasionally—if we're not too exhausted and really do need to nap—Michael and I try to go see a matinee Christmas afternoon in between family visits, *if* the timing works out. But in twelve years of marriage, I think we've only gone to a movie a couple times on December 25.

Oh well. There's always next year.

If you're having trouble carving out some alone time together, just the two of you, at Christmas, our English friend Pat has a surefire solution.

"No more Christmases being the place where everyone comes for lunch," she says. "Tell them that you are a vegetarian. Really, it works like a charm, especially if you throw in words like 'tofu' and 'quorn.'

"Seriously, a vegetarian Christmas is much more interesting than the same old same old that is served in most households," Pat says. "Last year our Christmas was on a Mexican theme. And our neighbors had a Caribbean Christmas. We found them sitting out in the conservatory in their most colorful shorts and T-shirts with the table covered in a whole range of exotic fruits and vegetables. Strangely enough, they do not seem to get any unwanted visitors."

Although Pat has a point, I don't think I could go without my traditional ham or turkey on Christmas Day.

Besides, I can't even say "quorn," much less know what it is.

Twosome Tip

Make sure you carve out some special "alone" time together as a couple during the holidays—even if you have kids. Ask a friend or family member to baby-sit so you can enjoy a movie, dinner, long walk, or even some last-minute shopping.

It's important to connect with each other during the craziness of the season and to focus just on each other.

Christmas party ideas and fun ways to avoid common party pitfalls.

12

That's the Couple Who Rocks

We do not remember days, we remember moments.

Cesare Pavese

I (Michael) am not really comfortable at parties. Unless I have something to do. Give me a game to play or a function to fulfill and I'm a happy camper.

Especially if it's a game.

Over the years, Laura and I have perfected some great party games. One of our favorites is the white-elephant gift exchange at Christmas. Everyone brings a wrapped gift, we draw numbers, and when our numbers come up we can either open a new gift or steal something someone has already unwrapped. If your gift is stolen, then you get to choose a new gift or steal someone else's. Fun when done the traditional way, but even better with our modifications.

Though called the "white-elephant" gift exchange, perhaps that's not the best nomenclature. Historically, the term came from Asia, where such a gift was actually a burden rather than a blessing. Since white elephants were sacred, they could never be put to work. Whoever received one was then obligated to feed and care for the animal throughout its extremely long lifetime (elephants live about as long as humans). Quite a financial drain.

By white-elephant exchange, we now mean that the presents given are garage sale–type items. Not something you purchase, but something you have around the house that you don't want anymore.

We tell people—either on the invitations or directly— that it's more fun if you bring something that someone might actually want to steal. One year I opened papier-mâché fruit. It was obvious that no one would want to steal it, so I watched from then on, knowing that, for me, the game was over.

We already told you about our friend Tom receiving a prune when he was in the Boy Scouts. Even worse for us was the year somebody brought a partially eaten hamburger. I'm totally serious. We were there. It really did happen.

On the other hand, one year at another friend's white-elephant exchange, there were several gifts worth stealing. One in particular was a beautiful handcrafted 8 x 10 framed paper cutting of the Nativity. The game was very exciting as the presents bounced from person to person. Trouble was, they kept bouncing and it seemed the game would never end. So the next year we came up with the rule that any particular gift could be stolen only three times. Whoever gets it on the third steal knows they get to keep it.

It is wonderful when you have a group that gets together year after year. Gifts have a habit of returning to the exchange. With the group mentioned above, there was an old 1950s science textbook. One couple, Mark and Andrea, got it the first year, we ended up with it the second year, and I brought it back for the third. That was the year the recipient read the inscription out loud. Laura (yes, my wife, the writer) was impressed that it was signed by the author and was very surprised that I would have given it away. Autographed books, even if they are out-of-date technical tomes, are still precious.

Then I admitted that it was me who signed the book with the author's name. So much for precious.

But it did get a great laugh.

Then there is Chuck and Nela's white-elephant exchange. Nela is my quilting mentor, and while she and her husband don't have a Christmas party every year, it's a nice reunion of the same core of people plus many new friends, and we have a great time. One year one of the ladies opened a gift and was more than a little embarrassed to find herself the recipient of a black lace teddy.

We're not talking just any teddy. We're talking Frederick's of Hollywood, over-the-top tacky teddy.

The next year the tacky teddy was back and was opened by one of the husbands. The year after that, it came back stuffed into a jelly jar. We all suspected that "Teddy" must be in one of those packages, but no one expected it to be in *that* package.

Homemade preserves, yes. Teddy, no.

The white elephant is a great game for ten or more people. We've played it with over twenty, but remember, the more players, the longer it will take to complete. We once played it with only four couples. Since we all knew what we and our spouses had brought, it was rather limited pickin's, but it was more controlled. Laura opened a big flat present that turned out to be a three-foot-wide watercolor print of Victorian ladies in a garden, beautifully framed and matted. She was thrilled.

But then it was stolen.

But then it was my turn. Stolen back.

The woman who brought the gift actually apologized for giving the print. She'd liked it when she bought it, but she and her husband had never hung it since it didn't go with the rest of their more contemporary home. We, on the other hand, immediately hung it in our bedroom. It's still there, and we often look at it and remember our wonderful friends and that white-elephant exchange.

A great variation is to have the same type of game but with Christmas ornaments. I've done this a few times at work, with the ornaments both wrapped and unwrapped. Wrapped makes for much more surprise, but unwrapped allows everyone to see all the ornaments and choose the one they like the best—great for people who have a theme to their holiday decor. Again, we limit the stealing to only three times per ornament.

Speaking of work, secret Santas are a great way to celebrate the season at the office. For those of you not familiar with secret Santas, let me explain. Everyone's name goes into a hat, and each person draws one. You are that person's secret Santa and do things for them for the established period of time. Santas are revealed on the last day of the game.

Because some people go overboard and do too much, and others are overwhelmed and do nothing, we've found it helpful to be very specific with the guidelines. They are meant to be freeing rather than constricting. To allow everyone to have fun and to avoid hurt feelings among recipients. (See sidebar.)

We found it was helpful to have someone from another unit in our building who knew who was assigned to whom. She also filled in as "Elf" to make special deliveries during work hours. I think she may have had more fun than those of us playing the game.

Then on the last day possible before people leave for the holidays, have a special meeting where everyone has to guess who their Santa is.

Although Laura and I don't do secret Santas at home—kinda hard to keep it secret when there's only two—we do hold a Christmas Eve open house every year for both sides of the family and a few special friends. Hearty homemade soups and crusty breads, hot apple cider, and eggnog. Simple fare and not a lot

Secret Santa Guidelines

- The game starts the Monday after Thanksgiving and ends on December 21.
- You should not spend more than ten dollars for the entire month.
- Look for inexpensive or free things.
  - Buy stocking stuffer–type toys
  - Leave special voice-mail messages
  - Send Christmas cards
  - Cut pictures out of holiday catalogs and tape them around your recipient's desk or computer
  - Have a spouse or child handwrite a note—the recipient will never recognize the writing that way
  - Decorate the recipient's desk with Christmas bows
  - Send a holiday helium balloon
  - Give homemade (or gourmet store-bought) cookies or brownies
- You should do no fewer than two things per week and no more than three.
- Remember to keep your identity a secret from everybody!

of sweets—we're usually "sweeted out" by then anyway. But Laura always makes sure to provide some of her fresh-baked Christmas cookies for those who might not have gotten their fill of sweets yet.

And for all who are able to stay, our newest craze—Christmas crackers. Think of a cross between a Christmas stocking and a piñata. This very English tradition is starting to catch on here in the States, and crackers are now available at more than just the import stores.

A cracker is like a paper-towel tube wrapped in gaily colored paper and twisted at each end like the cellophane around a piece of peppermint candy. Inside are a couple of toys, a silly joke, and a goofy crown-shaped crepe-paper hat. To open the crackers, you pull on each end. Here comes the scary part. Inside each cracker is a teeny-tiny firecracker "cap" that pops when you open it.

Sue and Rodger, our friends from England who own a bed-and-breakfast in Sutter Creek, California, explained that they played the crackers like a turkey wishbone. Two people each grab an end and tug on the same cracker until it bursts. Whoever ends up with the biggest end of the wrappings, gets the toys inside.

Pat and Dave, our other English friends, who still live in England, shared their variation of the wishbone idea. Everyone stands in a circle, crossing arms in front of their chests and tugging the crackers all at the same time.

It's absolutely hysterical to see us Yanks try to yank them this way. We still have not quite gotten the hang of it.

But there's always next year.

Even my ninety-year-old grandma donned her crepe-paper cap and read her riddle. And we have the photos to prove it.

Katie's Creamy Potato Soup Recipe

Our country friend Katie Young—who makes everything from scratch—gave us this great recipe years ago. She likes to add stewed tomatoes, but we prefer it without. We serve it every Christmas Eve, and people can't get enough of it.

3 cups cubed potatoes
½ cup diced celery
½ cup minced onion
½ cup carrots cut into slices

Put all vegetables in 2½ cups of water with ½ teaspoon salt. Cover and cook.

Cheese Sauce:
½ to 1 cup cheese (shredded cheddar or whatever your preference)
1 cup milk
4 Tbsp. butter
¼ tsp. salt
4 Tbsp. flour

Melt butter in pan at low heat. Add flour and salt to butter and mix until smooth. Slowly add 1 cup of milk, stirring constantly. When it thickens, remove from burner and add cheese. Once melted, add cheese sauce to water and vegetables. (We always double the recipe for our party.)

Delicious served with crusty French or sourdough bread.

Let the decorating decathlon begin!

13

Less Isn't Always More

All decorating is about memories.

Mrs. Henry ("Sister") Parish

Michael may be the "crafty" one in our family—able to create something beautiful out of next to nothing—but *I'm* the one who knows how to display it.

Just call me the decorating diva.

It satisfies my little homemaking soul to make things pretty and to hang them in just the right spot, whether it's Michael's gorgeous quilts, a small watercolor painting, or the English floral china plates I pick up at flea markets and garage sales.

But I don't consider myself a collector. Not in the least.

Doesn't every civilized home have seventeen teapots?

Michael, on the other hand, is the king of collectors. And his biggest collection involves his Father Christmases. But I think he's already written a whole chapter on that, so I won't repeat it here.

Suffice it to say that when we decorated for our first Christmas together and he pulled out box after box of Father Christmases, I was a little, um, overwhelmed. Where in the world were we going to display all of them? Never fear.

The decorating diva gene kicked in, and I covered every imaginable surface with Father Christmases— kitchen counters, bookcases, end tables. I even put a trio representing different countries on the back of the commode. And every time I flushed I thought I detected the faint hum of bagpipes.

We kept the top of the entertainment center free of Father Christmases, however, because that was a place of honor reserved for the large ceramic Nativity set that Michael's mom had made him.

When we finally moved into our own house, I thought that at last we'd have plenty of room for all of our Christmas decorations.

Think again.

In those few years, the Father Christmases had multiplied like rabbits, so we were still hard-pressed to find enough room to display them all. The good news is that by now we'd instituted a tradition of starting our holiday decorating the day after Thanksgiving, so that gave me plenty of time to squeeze in all the little white-bearded guys *somewhere* before December 25.

I always enjoy finding just the right spot for everything.

Usually we put his mom's Nativity on the mantel, but one year we put it on the top of the old spinet piano instead, and I wove in pieces of fir and evergreen around the base.

That same year I decided I wanted an elegant mantel like the one I'd seen in a home decorating magazine—with nothing but fresh Christmas greenery and cream-colored candles of varying shapes and sizes. I pictured how beautiful it would look with all the candles lit and the scent of evergreen wafting into the room.

Until Michael nixed my idea.

He was a little "uncomfortable" with lit candles and highly flammable Christmas boughs.

Just because one year he lit his grandmother's mantel on fire when he tried to put a tabletop Christmas tree into the crackling fireplace. A branch got caught on the metal screen and exploded in a shower of flames that shot as high as the five-foot mantel, igniting the boughs on top and sending flames licking their way up. In less than three seconds, there were flames from floor to ceiling. And Michael—a high school sophomore at the time—stood there saying, "Oh. Oh. Oh."

Now he was telling me, "No. No. No."

I didn't understand *why* I couldn't have my pretty candles. After all, no *serious* damage had occurred at his grandmother's house.

And the insurance had paid for the repairs.

But he was insistent. "Either you can have unlit candles and real boughs or lit candles and fake boughs. But you CANNOT have real boughs and lit candles."

So much for my elegant decorating dreams that year. After I mourned the loss of my pretty mantel vision for a few days, I finally went out and bought some fake greenery.

That never caught on fire.

One season Michael decided to sell some of his projects at holiday craft fairs. The biggest hit—next to his handmade pearl-and-bead ornaments—were two-foot by two-foot quilted wall hangings of pretty Christmas trees or wreaths.

Everyone oohed and aahed over the intricate work, and family members eyed them covetously. That year several members of our immediate family—and a couple of near and dear friends—received them as presents.

It was only afterward that I realized *our* home didn't have one of the wreath hangings.

But that crafty guy of mine remedied that in short order. He had seven leftover individual wreath panels that he hadn't yet made into finished wall hangings, so wanting to do something special for me, he quickly dashed off two more wreath "tops" on the sewing machine and stitched all nine together to form one giant wall hanging.

I so enjoy reaping the benefits of being married to a talented Renaissance man.

Another decorating treasure I look forward to putting out every Christmas is a beautiful wreath my sister Lisa gave us. Knowing how much Michael and I love roses, she commissioned a wreath-making friend to include some pretty burgundy silk roses along with the Victorian decorations and a little gold angel on top. We love it. Thanks again, Lee.

But the decoration that holds the most significance for me is a twelve-inch "jewel tree" my mom made many years ago.

My Grandma Florence—Mom's mother-in-law—in addition to being a great cook and baker, also loved to sew and make wonderful crafts. Her jewel trees were especially beautiful. As a little girl, I was transfixed by the way they sparkled and glittered in the light.

She created the trees from bits and pieces of mismatched costume jewelry that she kept in an old cigar box—a rhinestone earring here, a garnet brooch there, a pretend sapphire that had long ago fallen out of its inexpensive ring setting, and all of it mixed in with pearls and gleaming beads from broken necklaces.

Grandma would affix these pretty fake gems and jewels to a Styrofoam cone with straight pins and glue, constantly turning the cone in the light to make sure every inch of Styrofoam was covered. Then she'd spray paint a small ice-cream sundae glass gold for the base of her creation and glue the glittering tree to the top of it.

She made trees for both her daughters and daughters-in-law, and my mom proudly displays hers every Christmas.

But Grandma Florence passed away before she had a chance to make any for her granddaughters, and we were a little too young to fully appreciate them at the time anyway. So years later when we were adults, my mom painstakingly made both Lisa and me jewel trees, copying Grandma's pattern.

And every Christmas that I set mine out and admire the beautiful stones sparkling in the light, I think of my grandma. And my mom.

Thanks, Mom.

Grandma's daughter, my Aunt Sharon, likes to decorate her home with the Dickens Village every Christmas. She's become quite the collector—even attending seminars and compiling notebooks about her hobby.

Yet she's not a purist. She'll happily incorporate figures from other collections if she likes them better—like the covered bridge from the New England series.

Although I don't collect any of the Christmas village scenes, I *love* to decorate, and when it comes to Christmas—and living with Mr. Christmas himself—we usually go all out, negating the less-is-more effect I try to follow the rest of the year.

Okay, Mom, Lana, and Sheri—and anyone else who's ever set foot in our house—you can stop laughing now. What can I say? My natural fragrance is Eau de Clutter.

But one November I was on a major book deadline, Michael was heavily involved in the church Christmas play, and I didn't have the energy for our annual decorating decathlon.

That year we opted for the less-is-more look and scaled wa-a-ay back. We still put up both Christmas trees, but we reduced the Father Christmas collection to Michael's top ten favorites. The only other decoration was his mom's beautiful Nativity.

Now, that was a nice, peaceful Christmas. I wasn't frantic or harried, and it wasn't a major decorating production that took multiple days to accomplish.

The next year, however, we discovered we'd missed seeing many of our treasures, so we hauled them all out again from the garage rafters.

Patricia, our English friend, tells of the time a few years ago when she and her family went out for a special meal during the holidays. "The paper Christmas napkins were gorgeous, so my sister-in-law swiped some from another table and put them in her handbag," she recalled.

"They were a little creased by the time she got them home, so she ironed them. I think she was probably a little the worse for wear, because she did this on the carpet. As a result, she had to move the furniture around to cover a curious patch of blurred holly leaves and berries."

Hmmm. Carpet decorating. That's one area of the house I hadn't considered . . .

Decorating Tip

If you're generally from the less-is-more school of decorating, Christmas may be the time to let your inner clutter bug out. Be free! Be wild! Go crazy! And if you can't go crazy, then go simple instead and only display the things that mean the most to you.

The yearly Christmas lights saga.

14

Up on the Housetop

Let your light shine before men.

Matthew 5:16

We bought our house in October. And I (Michael) couldn't wait to decorate for Christmas.

White lights lining the roof, windows, garage door, and all the bushes. But I drew the line at actually climbing on the roof. My boss at the time had fallen off his ladder the year before and fractured his arm so badly he came to work for months with a metal brace and pins sticking through his skin.

As much as I love the twinkling of little lights, it takes more than that to get me up on the housetop.

Besides, our roof is not very architecturally interesting. It's a rectangle. Four straight lines interrupted only by a chimney off one side.

In our fantasies, we envision owning our dream house—a two-story house with Victorian gables, turrets, and cupolas. Or adding a second story to our current house. Of course, we would have two or three dormer windows sticking out through the roof. Wouldn't the twinkle lights look great lining everything?

I have to work out the rooftop thing though. Somehow.

A few years back when those icicle lights came on the market, Laura and I decided to make the change and line the front of the house with them. I trotted down to the hardware store and came home with the shimmering booty. Upon opening the boxes, I found the lights all bunched up. The dangling parts went zigzag and didn't hang down very far. So I fixed them. I straightened all the zigs. Now the icicles hung long and straight.

All was fine until nightfall. Laura took one look and said, "What's wrong with the lights?"

"Nothing. What do you mean?"

"Look at the way they're hanging."

"Yeah? So, what's wrong with them?"

"They're hanging funny. They're supposed to be kind of zig-zaggy."

The next year we went back to the single strand of miniature twinkle lights.

But the year after that we finally did it right. When the electrician came to wire in our new sprinkler system,

I had him install extra sockets right next to the garage door. Just for the Christmas lights. And with the new electrical sockets, I was able to set it all up on a timer. What could be simpler? Well, it was time for icicles again, so we tossed the set that I had "fixed" and bought some new ones.

On sale.

That kept short circuiting.

That was the year we pretended.

During the daytime everyone could see the dangling wire cords. After dark we hoped everyone would think we just forgot to plug the lights in.

For as much as we love to decorate, especially at Christmas, I'm not that big on the outside decorations. Must be that ladder thing.

Last year, weary of the icicle wars, I finally succeeded in talking Laura into a single string of the big old-fashioned lights. The ones with bulbs bigger than my thumbs.

The look is clean and classic. Sleek and elegant.

At this writing, it's nearing the end of June. My lights are still there. Hanging right where I put them last December.

We were really good about putting all the other decorations away on New Year's Day. Got everything packed and stowed on the rafters in the garage. But that was a pretty full day, and we were both really tired afterwards and never made it out to the front yard.

I thought I'd get around to it the next weekend.

Then the next.

Or the next.

121

I'm glad I'm married to a woman who doesn't worry about those kinds of things.

"They're clear," Laura says. "Who can see them? If they were colored lights, it would be another matter. Besides, this way we're all set for our Christmas-in-July party."

Another less expensive, fun, and more flexible-on-the-schedule option is driving around looking at *other* people's Christmas lights during December—something we try to do at least once every season. Sometimes we'll take Gracie along with us. Not impressed with the sparkles, she's just happy for the ride and the company—especially if she sees another doggy she can bark at through the window.

Speaking of impressive, every year our newspaper puts out a special section with maps to the areas that have gone the extra kilowatt with their outdoor decorating.

There's one court in particular that we like to visit. Complete with traffic directors, all cars are instructed to turn out their headlights. With a speed limit of around five miles per hour, there's not much danger. Besides, with all the lights on the houses, who needs headlights to see?

Fabulous decorations, and not just lights. There are life-size figures of the holy family, angels, Santa, and once, even Elvis. It's better than the Electric Light Parade. Some homes are reverent, some fanciful, some even bordering on tacky in their exuberance.

On the latter, I agree with Laura's adage that less would be more.

One house that I always like is at the end of the block. Several years ago they added a second story to the house, with dormer windows jutting through the front of the roof. Rumor has it that the main reason the family remodeled was not because of the added space, but so they'd have a better facade for the Christmas decorations.

With all the competition on that court, I tend to believe it.

Because of the traffic, you kind of have to go with the flow. Sometimes I want to look longer at one house and less at another. So we've been known to park on the main street and walk through instead. One year we were walking through with several friends and decided to do some impromptu caroling. We stood there on the sidewalk and sang. Some of us had been in choir, so we sang the harmonies. Cars rolled down their windows; residents came out to listen or even join in. It was a very special moment that could not have been planned.

One of our favorite decorated houses is just a couple miles down the street from us. A large, two-story, classic brick mansion owned by a well-to-do local developer and his family, this beautiful home with classic lines and a gabled roofline looks like something out of a fairy tale.

It's the epitome of elegance, with white lights running along every line of the entire two-story structure; I wonder how long it took him to put up *his* lights. Wait a minute. What am I thinking? Of course he had his own electrical crew to go up on the housetop.

But I know that coveting my neighbor's roofline isn't kosher, so I resign myself to doing the best I can with what we've got—rectangular roof and all. Besides, I've figured out a way to punch it up a bit. Now I line the inside of all our street-facing windows as well.

Elegant, illuminating, and best of all, no "up on the housetop" involved.

Lighting Tips

If you're like me and don't like ladders, check out your neighbors' decorations. Who does good rooftops? Befriend them. Offer to bake cookies or wrap presents for them in exchange for their climbing prowess.

In business language, we call this a win-win.

Holiday stories from our four-footed family members.

15

Here Comes Doggy Paws, Here Comes Kitty Claws

If you have men who will exclude any of God's creatures from the shelter of compassion and pity, you will have men who deal likewise with their fellow men.

Francis of Assisi

Don't you just love to hear the pitter-patter of little feet around the house?

We do—even when the pitter-patter is more of a click-click-click of doggy paws on our hardwood floors.

Since Michael and I don't have children, our American Eskimo dog, Gracie—Princess Grace Elizabeth, to be precise—has become our canine "daughter." And this darling daughter adds a whole new dimension of joy to the holidays I'd never known before.

The first Christmas we had her—two months after we brought her home from the rescue shelter—we gave her a couple of special doggy bones and a squeaky stuffed animal, unwrapped, for her Christmas "presents."

Never having had a dog of my own before, I (Laura) was a little uncertain about the whole present thing at first. I mean, come on. Presents? For a dog?

But she's not "just a dog"; she's a member of our family.

Besides, Michael—who's had several dogs as pets throughout his life and knows them much better than me—insisted that she'd get her feelings hurt if she didn't get something while we were opening all our gifts.

Feelings hurt?

I had a lot to learn about animals.

But Michael was right. Dogs *do* have feelings—at least Gracie does. When she's sad or worried, we can always tell because she does her "seal-pup" impression.

Gracie has fluffy white fur—she resembles a little white fox—with a black nose, big black eyes, and pointed ears—with a mind of their own—that stand up. But when we scold her or she's unhappy about something, her ears go straight back and down so that she looks like a baby harp seal.

Since we don't want any seal-pup sadness at Christmas, Gracie gets a couple of presents every year. One fun thing we've learned to do is to stuff her toys in gift bags sans tissue paper. We'll set the bag in front of her; she'll knock it over, poke her little head inside, and root around until she finds her new stuffed animal, which she grabs victoriously in her mouth.

Sometimes, though, she thinks *our* presents are for her. Especially the year Michael got me overstuffed Winnie-the-Pooh slippers.

Gracie watched expectantly with a possessive gleam in her eye as I unwrapped the large, fuzzy, gold-and-red slippers. The second I set them down, she lunged for HER gift and fastened her teeth on one of Pooh's ears, trying to drag the slipper away.

"No, Gracie! That's the *Mommy's* slipper," Michael corrected.

Huh? But you always give ME the animal toys! Not Mommy. Are you sure you're not confused?

"No, Gracie," Michael patiently explained. "See, your baa-baa lamb squeaks," he said, squeezing her new stuffed lamb for emphasis and waving it under her nose invitingly. "Mommy's slippers don't."

Gracie's ears perked up; she looked at Michael, then me, and then her new baa-baa lamb. In a flash she dropped the quiet and boring Winnie-the-Pooh and sprang for the noisy little lamb instead—squeaking to her heart's content for the next ten minutes.

Until we distracted her with her stocking and the treats inside.

Our friends Dave and Pat, in England, who, like us, don't have any children, are the "parents" of Peanut the beagle and Pluto the shepherd–border collie mix.

Animals as Christmas Presents

What could be cuter than a new puppy or kitten under the tree? An adorable new pet is a gift that keeps on giving, right?

Yes. And then some.

Owning a pet is a ten- to twenty-year commitment with daily responsibilities and ongoing expenses. Not something that should be taken lightly or be expected of someone else. Thousands of unwanted animals wind up in shelters every year, the Society for the Prevention of Cruelty to Animals (SPCA) cautions. There are many factors to be considered: breed (temperament), size, personality, and age of the animal. Plus, is the potential pet a good match for the intended owner? Is December, with all the holiday stresses, really a good time to introduce a new member into the household? Check with your local SPCA before making such an important decision. Also, a great alternative would be to wrap a toy dog or cat along with a "gift certificate." Offer to research with the person what type of animal would be best for them and then go with them to the local SPCA or animal shelter to help pick out a pet after the holidays when life is back to normal.

They put up an advent calendar every year—a small wall hanging in festive fabric with little pockets that each have a date marked on them—and they'll put two doggy treats in each pocket and count down to Christmas Day that way.

"You have to hang it quite high on the wall, mind!" cautions Pat.

Although Peanut and Pluto love their treats, they *don't* like the "bangs" in the Christmas novelty crackers Pat and Dave open every year, but Pat says the paper hats in the crackers definitely look better around the dogs' necks than on them.

We have a couple of "hats" we put on Gracie at Christmastime, too—one's a little red-and-white Santa hat with holes for her ears, and the other is a pair of reindeer antlers made of brown felt. But Gracie's not a hat girl, so they only last a few moments at best before she pushes them off with her paws.

She doesn't seem to mind the red velvet bow that we attach to her collar though. I think it's that princess thing.

Our friends Lonnie and Joe have a couple of princesses in their house, too. Of the kitty-cat variety.

Kit-Kat and Lucy pretty much rule the roost in their lovely Michigan farmhouse.

Photos of these feminine felines even grace the Christmas tree, inside some lovely wooden ornaments Joe bought Lonnie one year. But lest you think the kitty cats selfish, let me assure you that the girls know proper etiquette. At Christmastime, they send Kit-Kat candy bars to everyone for presents.

My sister-in-law Sheri has loved cats for as long as she can remember, including the one who showed up at the family's door when she was a teenager. She named the cat "Stray Elizabeth," or rather, "Stray Elizabeth Victoria Catherine Crestworthy the Ninth."

Today she has a beloved white, fourteen-year-old cat named Sno Pink who is her "companion" when she wraps gifts.

"Pink likes to help wrap, so she'll lay on the paper while I'm rolling it out, or go inside the gift boxes," Sheri says. She's also been known to scramble up the tree a few times, but then that's one of the hazards of owning a cat.

Our friend Marian has found a way to break her cat of that habit.

When she first got Nessie, a beautiful silver tabby, she noticed that her new kitty—like most cats—was trying to get on the tree and play with the ornaments. So Marian gently picked up Nessie and carried her to the front of the tree, where she held her and stroked her and murmured sweet endearments, but when Nessie reached out to grab an ornament or bat at the tree, Marian said, "BAD kitty!" in a loud voice and gently swatted her paw. Nessie tried two or three times to bat at the tree, and each time Marian would say "BAD kitty!" and lightly tap her paw.

Nessie now steers clear of the Christmas tree, and Marian doesn't have to worry about broken ornaments.

She makes sure to get Nessie some special presents at Christmas though.

Animal gift giving isn't a one-sided affair, however. Gracie likes to give presents to her mommy and daddy, as well as to all of her canine and feline family members and friends in the neighborhood.

She started out small—just giving out treats to her kitty cousins Pink, Muffin, and Mr. Spitz; her grandma's little Chihuahua mix, Lacey; and the whole canine gang at Great-Grandma Adelaide's.

But then she felt bad 'cause she hadn't given anything to her friend Jake who lives across town, who'd given her a present the year before, or Haley, her pretty golden retriever friend across the street, so we added them to her gift list.

But the year Michael assembled Christmas packages for every one of Gracie's neighborhood friends and the two of them trotted off happily to deliver them, I finally put my foot down.

"Twenty-two dog presents is *too* much!"

Four-Footed Hint

So maybe you're not one of those people who goes overboard at Christmas with your pets, making them stockings or wrapping presents for them. Even so, it's nice to do a little something "extra" for—or from—your four-footed family members.

If you need an idea for something from the pet, how about a book on animal psychology? Or any kind of pet-related book. Last year, Gracie got me a book on why dogs are better than cats.

The making of a white Christmas and other holiday alternatives.

16

Away in a Ski Lodge

Love came down at Christmas,
Love all lovely, Love divine;
Love was born at Christmas;
Star and angels gave the sign.

Christina Rossetti

Thanksgiving Day 1989 found me (Michael) in a bad mood.

Two months into my new job working on a cruise ship, I had made a few friends. And Alan, my best friend from college, was my boss, so I was hardly alone. But still, this was Thanksgiving—an American holiday—and I was in international waters. I *felt* alone.

So rather than spending the afternoon with my shipmates, I spent it with Schwarzenegger. Barricading myself in my cabin, I watched Arnold's latest film on the ship's TV system.

And felt miserable and homesick.

When it was time for dinner, I glumly made my way to the mess hall and ordered pizza. That's when our cook—from Germany—looked at me perplexed.

"Aren't you American?" he asked.

"Yeah."

"Would you not like turkey?"

I couldn't believe it.

We were an international crew. The officers were Norwegian, the stewardesses were Scandinavian, the deck crew was Filipino, and the dining-room servers were Mediterranean. Only the entertainment department—about twenty of us in a crew of five hundred—was from the United States.

And yet our kind galley staff prepared Thanksgiving dinner for us.

"Of course I would like turkey. Thank you very much."

It really shouldn't have surprised me. Sure, we were an international crew, but about 80 percent of the passengers were from the United States. Naturally, the chefs on a cruise ship, where food is a favorite all-day and all-night activity, would prepare the Thanksgiving spread you might expect.

My afternoon was wasted in lonely isolation. True, I was not in my normal surroundings, comforted in my known traditions, but it was still a holiday.

And I could still celebrate.

That evening I joined a half dozen or so other Americans as we crammed into a tiny cabin to watch *My Fair Lady*, eat popcorn, laugh, and have a great time.

This was to set the tone for the next several weeks of celebrating.

When I joined the ship, I'd wisely decided to limit myself to only the amount of luggage I was physically able to carry—four bags. None of which included any of my holiday decorations.

At Christmastime we were in the Caribbean, and I found a Walgreen's on St. Thomas, one of the U.S. Virgin Islands. Of course, they had a Christmas section, so I bought a few strands of lights, some tinsel garland, and an eighteen-inch fake tabletop Christmas tree with miniature ornaments.

The lights and garland encircled my cabin, outlining the ceiling, doorway, desk, TV, and porthole. Various other decorations were placed in strategic spots to complete the room. Everybody commented how much they enjoyed my cabin because it was so festive.

A few of us decided to do secret Santas. Three men each drew the names of one of three women and vice versa. I drew Julie, the social director. Once when she was in her cabin getting ready for dinner, I stealthily plastered the outside of her door with figures of Santa and his reindeer.

Surprise!

I thought it would be fun to give her my favorite holiday book, *The Best Christmas Pageant Ever* by Barbara Robinson. It's the story of the Herdmans, who were "absolutely the worst kids in the history of the world,"

135

and how they manage to muscle their way into all the leading roles in the church Christmas pageant.[3] Hilarious, and yet poignant, it gives us fresh perspective on what it must have been like that first Christmas.

Trouble was, almost everyone knew how much I loved this book, so giving it to her would betray my secret Santa identity.

The solution? I bought a copy for each one of the ladies. No need to be secret, and this way they all benefited.

On Christmas Eve I talked one of the German desk clerks into giving me a key to Julie's cabin so I could deliver her stocking. When I explained what we were doing, he readily agreed, even though it was against the rules to give out keys to other cabins.

Elves come not only in different sizes, but also from different countries.

I'd been working all month on Julie's stocking (remember my stocking fetish?), and I imagined her surprise when she came "home" and found that Santa doesn't need a chimney to deliver presents.

But I wasn't prepared for her reaction.

Since she didn't get off work until after midnight, we didn't meet up until the next morning.

On Christmas morning, Julie shared how much she loved her stocking and told me she had sobbed when she opened up the Scotch tape. "My mama and daddy always put tape in my stocking," she said.

Proving that even though we grow up on the outside, there's still a little kid inside every one of us.

136

I (Laura), on the other hand, was always in a big hurry to shed that little kid. I couldn't wait to grow up, see the world, and become a cosmopolitan woman. That's why I joined the Air Force after high school—and pretty soon I was winging my way to Europe, where I spent some memorable years.

Including several Christmases.

There was one Christmas dinner that especially stands out in my memory.

My roommate Diane—also in the Air Force—and I had both been invited to family events by our respective American bosses, but eager to be on our own and not wanting to feel like third wheels, we had politely declined these familial offers.

We agreed that we'd simply enjoy a traditional English Christmas dinner at the village pub across the street from our little 350-year-old pink stone cottage. After all, we were both sophisticated, intelligent women on our own in another country—we certainly didn't need a family to celebrate the holiday.

Besides, how fun—and different—to have Christmas dinner in a pub with the locals.

So Christmas morning we listened to a little Nat King Cole while we exchanged gifts over a leisurely "cuppa" tea and toast and gabbed about the guys we were currently interested in. Finally, just before lunchtime we walked over to the pub for our nice Christmas dinner.

That's when we learned the sad truth.

"Sorry luv, we're not serving any meals today—we're closing up early so everyone can celebrate Christmas dinner with their families," the kindly red-cheeked publican informed us.

Nothing at all? Not even a chicken pie or sausage roll?

Not even any bubble and squeak (sausage and potatoes)?

But the pub *did* have an assortment of crisps (potato chips) and candy bars to tempt our taste buds. Diane chose salt and vinegar; I picked sour cream and onion. And for dessert, two Kit-Kats apiece.

That's one Christmas dinner that will go down in history.

Diane had a much better Christmas six years later in Germany with her soon-to-be husband, Warren.

"We bought a small tree from the nearby Christmas tree lot and decorated it with ornaments we'd bought locally and from the BX [base exchange]," she recalled. "We cooked a nice ham, potatoes and gravy, veggies and salad, and bought wonderful brochen (rolls) from the nearby baker and a nice Black Forest gateau cake for dessert.

"There was always something to do overseas," she said, "even if it was just walking along the walkplatz (shopping area) when the stores were closed. They always had little stands set up selling potato pancakes with applesauce, bratwurst, and gluhwein (warm mulled wine) at Christmastime."

Then there are the friends who decided one year to take their kids skiing up at Lake Tahoe for Christmas. That way they didn't have to rush from one side of the family to the other in the space of a few hours and wind up frazzled and exhausted at the end of the day.

And one of the best things about skiing on Christmas Day? The slopes were deserted.

During the day they'd ski or snowboard, and at night they'd enjoy a wonderful dinner in the cozy lodge with a lovely fire blazing away in the fireplace. That year they got to have a fun and much more intimate Christmas doing something the whole family enjoyed.

And you know what? It was one of their best Christmases ever.

Sometimes going away for the holidays is the best thing you can do.

My friend Lonnie introduced me to Stephanie because she thought her best-selling novelist friend's special Christmas-away-from-home story was one we might want to include in this book.

She was right. Although I interviewed Stephanie, I also asked if she could jot down some of the details. She did that so eloquently that I'm going to let her tell the story here in her own words, with my thanks.

The First One without Dad
by Stephanie Grace Whitson

In our twenty-seven years of married life, Bob and I had taken care to establish traditions that would ensure that Christmas was the best holiday of the year for our family—one of the more unusual being that someone in our family always gets a box of dirt. Never mind the significance . . . you had to be there. It was just part of what it meant to be a Whitson. But as the four children (ages 21, 18, 15, and 12) and I faced Christmas 2001, no one cared about the box of dirt. Bob had gone home to be with Jesus the previous February.

Robert Whitson had been battling cancer for nearly six years. He was a great man, if you define "great" the way we did—he worked hard, he loved his kids, he loved his wife, he served his Lord faithfully, and he died well. He accepted terminal illness, and he fought a good fight. And he kept the faith. He departed from his own bed, with his children gathered around and his wife whispering in his ear that when he saw Jesus, he should go home with Him.

We had known for months that Bob was going to die. We had always known that when he died, he would take up residence in heaven. But knowing those facts did nothing to make us feel that this Christmas could possibly be anything more than a day to be *endured*.

Grief is a strange journey. Sometimes it leads us straight at the thing we dread, and that is good. We need to face down the monster and know we can do it. Sometimes we need to take a detour around the monster until we are stronger. Christmas was one of those times when I felt we all needed a detour. That most special of holidays without Bob loomed large and threatening and awful. Instead of anticipating, we wanted to run screaming the other way. In a way we did . . . albeit without the audible screams. Still, we ran—to another *kind* of Christmas.

It all began with a phone call. From Switzerland. Bob's niece Laura, an engineer for IBM, had been living in Geneva for two years. Laura has always been among the "favorite cousins" category in our family, and when she moved to Europe, we had discussed how wonderful it would be if the children could go visit. But Bob's illness precluded the fulfillment of that plan. Now Bob's illness was no longer a factor, and with airfare "in the basement," Laura was wondering if there was any way the children and I could spend Christmas with her?

No. I didn't think so.

Yes. Maybe.

Well, I would think about it and get back to her. Did she think that if we came to Geneva we might also be able to spend a few days in Paris? (I lived in France for a summer when I was in college, and I had always longed to return.)

Yes. Of course. Laura thought that would be fun. Just let her know.

I hung up the phone and contemplated all the obstacles. Getting anywhere from Lincoln, Nebraska, is never cheap. My two oldest children (ages 21 and 18) had jobs, and they wouldn't be able to get away. Besides that, they were both in love. They wouldn't want to leave for a week. And the money. Oh, the money.

As it turned out, getting to Geneva from Lincoln, Nebraska, was cheap. And the two oldest children wanted to go. And their bosses let them off. And my financial advisor agreed without hesitation that Bob would indeed approve of this use of a portion of his life insurance money.

And so on Christmas Eve, instead of going to church and blinking back tears because Daddy wasn't there and coming home to try to enjoy the traditional feast with that Daddy-sized hole in our hearts . . . we were in the air on our way to Geneva, Switzerland.

On Christmas Day, instead of stumbling into the Daddy-less living room and pretending to enjoy opening presents and eating the brunch he didn't cook at a table with The Empty Chair . . . we were fighting jet lag, walking the medieval streets of Geneva, eating dinner with an international group of Laura's friends. We met people from Switzerland, Sweden, and England. My Midwestern children loved it.

And then, the day *after* Christmas, we boarded the TGV train (its 180 mph speed impressed my boys) and were whisked away to Paris. Laura and I speak French. She had been to Paris before, and I lived in France for a summer during my college days. I adore Paris, and I couldn't wait to show it to my children.

Not many things elicit a *wow* from teenagers these days. When you've traveled to other planets via the movies, it's hard to be impressed. But standing in front of Notre Dame Cathedral, my son asked, "*When* did you say they built that?"

"In the 1200s."

He stepped closer to the doors, examining the myriad stone figures carved up and up . . . and up. . . . He stood back. "*Wow.*"

One night we rode the metro a short distance. Emerging out of the earth, we walked along the Seine, admiring a particularly beautiful bridge, watching a *bateau mouche* make its way up the river, wondering how much it cost to live in those apartments with that view of the city. Then we advanced beyond the row of trees shading the walkway along the apartment houses. The Eiffel Tower loomed above us in the night, its ironwork glowing bronze in the lights.

Wow.

One night we paused to investigate what was "inside" a tall iron fence around a city block we passed by every morning and every evening on the way to and from our hotel just across from the Sorbonne. Reading a sign, we learned we had been casually passing by third-century ruins of a Roman bath. Roman. As in Julius Caesar. As in togas and . . . *wow*.

We grabbed floor plans of the Louvre one day just before it closed, and that evening in our hotel room I told the children to look it over and mark what they really wanted to see. I didn't want their eyes to glaze over in a museum. I wanted them to see less and appreciate more—to remember more than hours of wandering a maze of marbled halls.

Upon arrival the next morning, we headed for the usual things: *The Winged Victory, Mona Lisa, Venus de Milo.* I had my daughter photograph a couple of floors as inspiration for future quilts. I watched my children watch. What would they really *see?*

It was the sculpture. Nebraska is known for many things. One of them is *not* Greek/Roman/Italian sculpture. My children were in awe. Their mother was delighted. *They are getting it . . . they really are getting it. . . .*

In those four days in Paris, we probably walked five miles a day. We didn't see the Musee d'Orsay. We didn't go up the Eiffel Tower. We didn't ride on a *bateau mouche* or go to the Cluny Museum or eat at a fancy restaurant or do any number of a zillion things tourists usually go to Paris to see and do. But we did climb the towers of Notre Dame and see the gargoyles. We did walk the streets of Little Athens and marvel over the array of foods in the restaurant windows. We did shop at La Samaritaine. We ate mussels and lamb and "steak frites" and crepes and lychees and discovered

Nutella chocolate. We shopped at an open-air market and made mistakes and got lost. We marveled at the traffic and the smallness of the cars (where would you ever park a pick-up?) and the beauty of the roses at the flower market.

Christmas 2001 was a gift. Four kids from small-town America wandered the streets of the most beautiful city in the world. "It changed everything," my eldest daughter, Brooke, said when we got back. "I'll never look at life the same way again." And then she said something else that warmed my heart. "Can we go back?"

Going Away Tip

If you need a change at the holidays—for whatever reason—consider going somewhere new and different this year. It doesn't have to be an expensive overseas trip either. Perhaps you've never seen the ocean and always wanted to. This is your chance.

Or maybe you've always dreamed of spending Christmas in a charming inn in New England. Go for it! Or maybe you like to "rough it" a bit . . . I hear there's plenty of simple, rustic cabins or campsites you can rent in the countryside or in and around national parks. I (Laura) wouldn't know for certain though, because "roughing it" isn't in my vocabulary. I suggest searching the web for state and national parks for further information.

I don't imagine we will ever spend Christmas in Paris again. But in 2001, being there helped one heartbroken family from Nebraska get past a milestone no family ever wants to face. On our first Christmas without Dad, we went to the City of Lights. Of course, Dad spent the day with the one who said, "Let there be light." But we did all right too. And you know what? We're going to *be* all right. We're already talking about who gets the box of dirt this Christmas.

How to brighten a child's Christmas.

17

Rent-a-Kid and Other Ways to Make the Yuletide Bright

I love little children, and it is not a slight thing when they, who are fresh from God, love us.

Charles Dickens

Whether you're single or married without kids, there's something special about spending time with a child at Christmas and seeing all the magic and wonder through their big, wide eyes. If you don't have a child, or if your children are grown, then we recommend renting one—niece, nephew, grandchild, neighbor, son or daughter of a friend—for a short time during the holidays.

"When my niece, Mackenzie, was three years old, my mom and I took her to a musical rendition of *A Christmas Carol*," said my friend Kim. "But it wasn't necessarily meant for young children, and we got some sideways glances. One patron was even so bold as to say, 'She's so young! Are you sure she won't get bored and make a fuss?'"

"We were sure," Kim said. "I'd swear she came out of the womb adoring anything on a stage. She'd already been to a couple of other theatrical performances, and each time was the same: enthralled, eyes wide, and not a peep out of her from beginning to end.

"That same year—and since Mackenzie is a Christmas baby, born on December 23—I thought what better way to celebrate than to take her to the *Nutcracker Ballet*? So we read her the story and introduced her to all the characters. It was all she could talk about for a week. Always in the Christmas spirit, I was looking forward to a little fairy dust myself.

"The evening of the performance went exactly as anticipated: enthralled, eyes wide, and not a peep from beginning to end. We were having so much fun we decided on a fancy dinner to top it off. I ordered an appetizer of steamed mussels," Kim said, "never dreaming that a three-year-old would want any. The next thing I knew, she'd rolled up her sleeves and was elbow-deep in the plate of mollusks! We laughed so hard we had to take a picture just to prove it to the rest of the family.

"Then and there we decided to make it a Christmas tradition—every year I take my niece to the *Nutcracker* and a fancy restaurant (but it must have steamed mussels on the menu). Last year we did this in San Francisco, and we dreamed about other cities we would eventually take our tradition to—London? Paris? Moscow? After all, the sugar plum fairy sprinkles her dust and makes Christmas magic all over the world. . . . Do they have mussels in Moscow?"

I'm not sure if they have mussels in Moscow, but I know they have Mel's Diner in Sacramento—or they did.

Mel's Diner and a matinee, or McDonald's and a matinee, were usually the entertainment of choice for my nephew Josh and me (Laura) during the Christmas season. We loved catching the newest children's comedy or action-adventure release at the theater.

For some reason he wasn't too interested in sugar plum fairies.

Josh remembers my taking him to a Mel's in our neighborhood that had '50s cars sticking out of the walls. You sat in car seats inside the retro diner while you downed your chocolate shakes and cheeseburgers.

This no-longer-young boy also seems to remember something about a burping contest in the car on the way home after seeing *Back to the Future*, but I'm sure he's mistaken. His Aunt Laura was too genteel, too refined, too much of a lady to do anything so gross and junior-highish as burp.

In public.

Another thing Josh liked to do around the holidays with me—and his mom and grandma—was bake Christmas cookies. Like most kids, he liked to make sugar-cookie cutouts that he could decorate to his heart's content. I seem to remember a giant purplish-brown Santa whose head he eagerly bit off before the frosting had even hardened.

There are also ways to brighten the life of a child you *don't* know during the holidays.

Christmas season starts in November for our friends Lesley and Kyle with their participation in the Samaritan's Purse Operation Christmas Child. This wonderful mission organization started several years ago by Franklin Graham—son of Billy—provides shoe-box gifts to thousands of children in need around the world—generally in third-world countries.

Lesley and Kyle have a blast choosing stuff for the shoe boxes.

"Last year we chose to buy for all boys," she said, "and Kyle especially had fun with this project. We went to the store and spent hours in the toy section, looking for what we thought a child of five might want, as well as a boy of eight, and a boy of thirteen. Kyle picked up all the action figures and told me stories of his childhood. Then he played with all the cars and looked longingly at the car kits that he said he always loved as a boy.

"This is truly our favorite time of gift wrapping and giving," Lesley said.

Ditto.

Michael and I have been filling the shoe boxes for several years now and it's a highlight of our holiday. It fills the need in my Mr. Christmas—the guy who's so big on Christmas stockings—to fill a container with small presents. Shoe boxes and stockings are equally fun to fill, he says. Plus it's great to know we're helping some children have a merry Christmas while meeting some very real needs.

We always try to include some basic toiletries—combs and brushes, small soaps, and toothbrushes and travel-size toothpaste—but then we quickly focus on the fun stuff that kids like to play with: coloring books and crayons, pretty barrettes, and hair ribbons for the girls; matchbox cars for the boys; and miniature stuffed animals for both.

It's fun to shop and find just the right balance between needs and wants.

My practical Michael says planning ahead makes good economic sense. We usually hit Target or Wal-Mart in August for the back-to-school sales for the crayons, pads and pencils, etc. And party supply stores like Michael's or even a dollar store are great for the small toys and games.

One added benefit of this program is that the shoe boxes are dropped off in mid-November—before Thanksgiving. It's a great way to start the season off right. In focusing on children who have so little, we find that we all the more readily acknowledge how truly blessed we are.

Then there are the kids in need in your own back-yard.

Many shopping malls in the community—often in conjunction with philanthropic organizations—have

Christmas trees set up in the center of the mall covered with paper "ornaments" that bear the name, age, and Christmas wishes of needy children in the area. You select one or more children's names from the tree, shop for the gift they requested, wrap it, and return it to the volunteers at the mall.

There are also church-sponsored programs, such as Chuck Colson's Prison Fellowship Angel Tree ministry that helps out children whose parents are incarcerated.

One of our friends summed it up best. "This is my special time for anonymous giving," she said. "I take great pains in choosing the angels from the tree and shopping for these gifts on my own. It's also my time of reflection—a look back with thanksgiving for all the privileges and blessings I had as a child that these children don't have."

There are many ways to bless children—and adults—less fortunate than us.

Michael's Aunt Betty tells the story of a young woman, "Mary," who worked in her office and didn't have a very merry Christmas to look forward to. A suddenly single mother of two soon to give birth to her third child, Mary's husband had just left her—taking almost everything she owned. Leaving her and the kids with practically nothing.

It was a difficult time, and looked to be a pretty lean Christmas for Mary's family. But her coworkers rallied around the young mom—as did anonymous members of Betty's church—and provided a Christmas turkey and all the trimmings, plus additional food to stock her cupboards, clothes and toys for the kids, odds and ends of furniture, a microwave, and some much-needed cash.

Mary couldn't believe it. That strangers would do all this for her! But then she realized that they were "angels" that God had sent to her and her family in their time of need.

Our family had angels arrive one Christmas, too.

The year I was fifteen, my dad died unexpectedly of a heart attack just two weeks before Christmas. Suddenly my mom was left with four kids to raise all on her own.

We'd just moved to Phoenix from Wisconsin a few months earlier, and even though we had relatives on my

Finding a Child in Need

For more information about Franklin Graham's Operation Christmas Child, check out their web site at www.SamaritansPurse.org. Or if you'd like further details on Chuck Colson's Prison Ministries Fellowship Angel Tree, the web site is www.angeltree.org.

If there's not a program sponsored by your favorite shopping mall, call your local fire department. Firefighters often have a Toys for Tots–type program, or they might at least know of one in your area.

mom's side of the family there, it was difficult to be in a new place for our first Christmas—especially without my dad. To help out, a nearby church brought over food, clothing, and Christmas gifts for each one of us.

And I've never forgotten their kindness.

My father was a big believer in the Golden Rule— "Do unto others as you would have them do unto you"—and he taught that rule to each of us kids.

That's why a couple years ago, Michael and I made the decision to change our gift giving. We used to give gifts to everyone in our respective families—even those we're not close to or don't see very often.

Until it got way out of control.

He's the youngest in a family of six children; I'm the second oldest in a family of six. All our siblings have children of their own—and most have spouses—and now most of *their* kids have kids, too. It got to the point that we were giving gifts to over fifty family members. Yikes!

We decided it was time to "stop the insanity."

So recently, we asked our relatives to stop giving us gifts, because we didn't really *need* anything. And we decided that the only family members we would continue to give Christmas gifts to were my mom and Michael's grandmother.

Now we take the money we would have spent on all those family members and instead "adopt" a family in the community that's really in need.

Other friends of ours do something similar.

Jan and Carl—who have a blended family of grown children—have recently asked their kids not to get them any Christmas presents from now on, but to instead make a donation to a charity like the Heifer Project, where they can buy a goat or a pig or some kind of animal for a family in a third-world country.

"At this stage, we really don't need anything," Jan said, "and this is a tradition that will make Christmas much more meaningful to us and be a relief to the kids at the same time."

We second that emotion.

Rent-a-Kid Tip

Do something to bring joy to the life of a child this Christmas. Whether that means taking a niece, nephew, grandchild, or neighbor out for a special holiday treat—like the Nutcracker or the latest Disney release—"adopting" a lonely child in the neighborhood, or buying gifts for a child in need whom you don't know, find a way to make the yuletide bright for a child.

Isn't this all about a baby in a manger? Bringing Christ back into Christmas.

18

What Child Is This?

He was created of a mother whom he created. He was carried by hands that he formed. He cried in the manger in wordless infancy, he the Word, without whom all human eloquence is mute.

Augustine of Hippo

Our beloved Charles M. Schulz put it on national television in 1965. In the midst of partying and distractions, Charlie Brown cries out, "Isn't there anyone who knows what Christmas is all about?"

"Sure, Charlie Brown." And Linus recites the Christmas story from the Bible—the Gospel of Luke:

And there were in the same country shepherds abiding in the field, keeping watch over their flock by night. And, lo, the angel of the Lord came upon them, and the glory of the Lord shone round about them: and they were sore afraid. And the angel said unto them, Fear not: for, behold, I bring you good tidings of great joy, which shall be to all people. For unto you is born this day in the city of David a Saviour, which is Christ the Lord. And this shall be a sign unto you; Ye shall find the babe wrapped in swaddling clothes, lying in a manger. And suddenly there was with the angel a multitude of the heavenly host praising God, and saying, Glory to God in the highest, and on earth peace, good will toward men.

Luke 2:8–14 KJV

Laura and I read these words each Christmas before we open our presents. It's one of our traditions. And it better helps us focus back on the one who made it all possible.

My sister and her family have a different tradition to achieve the same purpose. A "Happy Birthday, Jesus" cake, which they serve on Christmas Eve.

We acknowledge that December 25 is not the historic date of Jesus' birth. And that there are so many facets of our holiday season that do not directly apply to the birth of our Savior. Secular in the midst of the spiritual.

But still we celebrate.

Hopefully, with all of our hearts.

It's so easy to get distracted from the true meaning of Christmas, but there are many things we can do to keep the focus.

Where to Find the Christmas Story in the Bible

While much was foretold by Isaiah and the prophets about the birth of the Messiah, only two of the Gospels talk about it.

Matthew records a few paragraphs about the birth, but Luke gives us a lot more details, taking the whole first chapter to set things up. Chapter two describes the birth of Jesus and the visiting shepherds. This is the account most familiar to us, thanks, in part, to the Peanuts gang.

Christmas Eve church services are one such way. It is, after all, where we got the name—Christ mass.

Once we attended an unusual—at least for us—service. As we entered, each of the grown-ups was given an unlit candle. At one point in the service, all the lights were turned out and one solitary candle was lit in the back of the room. That candle bearer lit another person's candle, then that person lit another person's. And so the light spread throughout the room. It was a wonderful experience we will never forget.

Then we all proceeded out to the parking lot, where we formed a circle and sang carols accompanied by guitar. "Silent Night" has never been so personal as that night, bundled up in our coats, mist forming from our breath, and illuminated by the candlelight.

One pastor reads the same story every year about the misfit boy who was a little slower than the rest of the kids but who really wanted to be in the pageant. Finally, one year they cast him as the innkeeper. Not much trouble he could get into there, right? But when Joseph and Mary pleaded with him for a place to stay, instead of offering them the stable, he said, "It's okay, you can have *my* room."

A pageant with the unexpected makes you see the familiar in a different way. A new perspective.

Like in Barbara Robinson's hilarious book *The Best Christmas Pageant Ever,* which I mentioned in an earlier chapter. The Herdman children did not grow up in church and would be best described as little hoodlums. When they muscled their way into all the leading roles in the pageant, no one knew what to expect. Few things happened the way they were supposed to, but rather than ruin everything, it turned out to be the best pageant the church ever had.

Children being children. Is it any wonder that Jesus said, "For the kingdom of God belongs to such as these" (Mark 10:14)?

Christmas pageants can be great for reminding us about the Savior King and his humble birth.

In the chapter "Those Not-So-Silent Nights," I talked about the church pageants I was involved in. The evening always ended with a Nativity processional. When the size of the audience outgrew the size of the church building, we moved the production to an old historic theater downtown. It's a huge auditorium.

Mary and Joseph are onstage with the baby Jesus, and the kings with their entourage enter from behind the audience. Regal five-foot-tall banners on eight-foot-tall rods precede the Wise Men, proclaiming messages like "King of Kings," "Lord of Life," and "Alpha and Omega." Sometimes the Wise Men walk under canopies or are carried by servants on a kingly sedan chair. Sometimes even accompanied by live animals. They proceed up the center aisle like the bride at a wedding, accompanied by stirring music. It's grand and glorious. The audience always gasps, and many have been known to shed a tear or two. Or three.

On stage, the Wise Men join the holy family and present their gifts. Timed to the music, which now reaches its crescendo, on the final beat, all bow down to the babe in the manger.

Talk about the reason for the season.

One Sacramento church, Arcade Baptist, hosts its annual drive-through Nativity.

It's open to the public and free of charge, so people can experience the Christmas story without leaving their cars.

Meandering for maybe a half mile through the parking lot are individual set pieces showing the various scenes in the life of the Messiah. Live actors stand frozen like statues in the scenes while cars drive past. Sometimes frozen is more literal than figurative, as this is winter after all. Large signs explain the story, and Christmas music plays throughout.

In one early scene, we see the angel Gabriel appearing to the terrified Mary, announcing that she would give birth to the Son of God.

Another scene shows Mary and Joseph en route to Bethlehem for the census, and another shows Jesus lying in the manger.

But this pageant takes it further than usual. They show Jesus as a grown-up, beginning his ministry, offending the established leadership, dying on the cross, coming back to life on Easter morning, and ascending back up to heaven, where he is still alive today.

Now that's what I call focusing on the real meaning of Christmas.

Christ-mas Tip

No matter what your religious background—or lack thereof—pick a local church and attend a Christmas Eve service. Many churches advertise in the newspaper exactly what times they hold their services. Start times will probably range from the midafternoon until midnight, so there's bound to be something that fits your schedule.

Most churches are used to guests at this time of year and make the extra effort to be visitor-friendly. And if you already have a church you call your own, why not invite your neighbors or coworkers to attend services with you?

Our totally subjective and quasi-comprehensive list of who sings the best version of our favorite Christmas songs.

Encore

Sorrow, gladness, yearning, hope, love,
belong to all of us, in all times and
in all places. Music is the only means
whereby we feel these emotions in their
universality.

H. A. Overstreet

Something has been nagging at me (Michael) since we started writing this book, and no, it's not Laura. Where's the music?

We've talked about movies—and then some—and I mentioned the histories of a few songs, but that doesn't seem enough. After all, what is Christmas without carols?

Silent, as in night—which is also a carol.

Because of my former life as a professional singer and actor, I'm more familiar with performing stage shows than with writing books. That's how I got the idea for this encore. A concert is not over just because the band has sung their "last" song.

So why should a book be over just because we've ended the last chapter?

It made perfect sense to me that we could offer an encore and that it would be about music.

Granted, my wife/coauthor didn't see the connection at first—and it rather surprised our editor, too—but they quickly got into the groove.

So we're offering you an encore—because we can.

Music lovers that we are, we naturally have many Christmas albums. And naturally, we also have our favorite recordings. So Laura and I compiled a list of our favorite Christmas songs by whoever we think sings that particular song the best.

Granted, our choices were limited by our own CD and tape collection, and like all lists, it's totally subjective. You will no doubt disagree with some of our selections. Hey, we don't even agree on some of our selections, so we've listed both choices.

So here they are, randomly gathered within three sections: classic, novelty, and contemporary.

Part One—Classics

"White Christmas"—Bing Crosby. Come on, it's gotta be Bing. It's the top-selling single of all time, after all.

Our second favorite recording would have to be Bing's duet with Rosemary Clooney.

"Silver Bells"—also goes to Bing and Rosemary. It's rich, it's warm, it's classic.

"The Christmas Song" (Chestnuts Roasting on an Open Fire)—Nat King Cole. Another given. Nat was the first to record it and is still the best.

However, a close second is Linda Eder, a relative newcomer, who got her start on Broadway. No wonder we like her. A bit of Barbra Streisand, a bit of Celine Dion, with just enough Linda Ronstadt. Wow.

"Have Yourself a Merry Little Christmas"— Judy Garland. It's worth watching the whole movie *Meet Me in St. Louis* just to see Judy in that gorgeous red dress singing this beautiful song.

Second place goes to Linda Ronstadt for her soulful but powerful rendition, followed closely—at least, according to Laura—by Rosemary Clooney.

"I'll Be Home for Christmas"—Linda Ronstadt again. She's got a way with those '40s ballads. (Can you tell we're fans?)

"Silent Night"—split decision. For Michael it used to be opera diva Kathleen Battle, but now she has been surpassed by Linda Eder.

For Laura it's Barbra Streisand all the way. Underplayed, yet you know it's power under control.

"Do You Hear What I Hear?"—Hands down Linda Eder. With its *Lion King* orchestration and choir background, crank it up so you can *feel* the song tonight. This rendition is so fresh and alive, I almost put it into the contemporary songs section.

"Let It Snow"—Steve Lawrence and Eydie Gorme. They're great together.

"O Holy Night"—Celine Dion. Simple and pure. Need we say more?

Laura remembers Julie Andrews singing it wonderfully, too, but we didn't have it in our collection, so we can't officially list her.

"Joy to the World"—Julie Andrews. We do have this one on CD.

Laura says Andy Williams needs to be included here, too. It's a nostalgia thing—she remembers all those Christmas specials growing up.

"Toyland"—Doris Day.

"Little Drummer Boy"—Anne Murray.

"Sleigh Ride"—Amy Grant. Did anyone ever record this before Amy?

"What Child Is This?"—Charlotte Church. Though still a teenager, she has such a grown-up voice. After listening to her for the first time, you may be asking yourself, what child is *this?*

"The Star Spangled Banner"—Sandi Patty. Gives us chills. Yeah, I know it's not a Christmas song, but it *is* appropriate for our Christmas-in-July party.

"Ave Maria"—We couldn't decide. First we came up with Kathleen Battle. Laura says she's exquisite; I say cool. Recorded by virtually everyone who's ever done a Christmas album, the song works so much better with someone who's classically trained.

Which is why we also love it sung by Placido Domingo.

And Mario Lanza.

And Ronan Tynan of the Irish Tenors.

"The First Noel"—John McDermott, another of the Irish Tenors.

"I Wonder as I Wander"—Tie. Barbra Streisand and Linda Ronstadt.

"Hark the Herald Angels Sing"—the cast of *A Charlie Brown Christmas*. Okay, so Laura doesn't agree. But *I'm* writing this chapter. I added it—because I could.

Part Two—Novelty Songs

"Rudolph the Red-Nosed Reindeer"—Tie between Gene Autry and Burl Ives.

"Santa Claus Is Coming to Town"—Frank Sinatra. Cool. Big band swing.

"I Saw Mommy Kissing Santa Claus"—Wayne Newton. Yes, Wayne Newton.

"The Twelve Days of Christmas"—John Denver & the Muppets. Though a traditional song, as performed by this bunch, it's truly a novelty. Of course, Miss Piggy steals the show with her "five golden rings."

"Chipmunk Song" (Christmas Don't Be Late)—Who else? Alvin and the Chipmunks. We had to list it.

"The Chimney Song"—from the Twisted Christmas CD. Sung by a little girl about ten or so years old. Something's stuck in the chimney . . . it turns out to be Santa.

Part Three—Contemporary Songs

"**Mary, Did You Know**"—Kathy Mattea. Not the first to record it but arguably the best.

"**Christmas through Your Eyes**"—Gloria Estefan.

"**O Little Town of Bethlehem**"—Amy Grant. Though the lyrics are classic, her new music is definitely contemporary. We have recordings of two other melodies—the way it was originally written and the second version that we normally sing and hear. Amy's version is the best.

"**Angels We Have Heard on High**"—Michael W. Smith. Another rewrite of a classic. He actually calls it "**Gloria,**" but a rose by any other name . . .

"**No Eye Has Seen**"—Amy Grant and Michael W. Smith duet. Rather than the usual melody and harmony, they're singing two different songs in one. Overlapping, weaving in and out with the choir background. Truly glorious.

"**The Prayer**"—Charlotte Church and Josh Groban. Sure, it's not just a holiday song, but it was originally recorded by Celine Dion and Andrea Bocelli for her Christmas album. Though we have all four of their CDs, we think Charlotte and Josh sing it best. More passion. More purity.

"**The Bells of Saint Paul's**"—Linda Eder. It's really a remembrance of a past love, but it's set at Christmastime and in London. Beautiful. Worth the whole price of the CD.

"**Breath of Heaven**"—Amy Grant. Although, had my niece Jennifer recorded it, she could have easily bumped Amy. (See "Those Not-So-Silent Nights" for the full story.)

Our two favorite Christmas CDs? Linda Eder's *Christmas Stays the Same* and Linda Ronstadt's *A Merry Little Christmas*. Big surprise, huh?

So that's our show, er, I mean book. And now it's time for the curtain call.

We hope that whether you're single or married, with kids or without, we've shown you new and fun ways to make your grown-up Christmas season bright. Remember, it's never too late to have a happy childhood!

And if you've got a grumpy scroogeyman in your life, do something kind to take the bah out of his humbug (a plate of fresh-baked cookies and a mug of hot chocolate often does the trick) or any simple act of kindness to demonstrate the love of that babe in the manger.

May you all "have yourself a merry little Christmas." And as Mr. Dickens said, "May God bless us, every one."

Acknowledgments

No book is ever a solo effort—especially in this case, our first coauthored writing effort as a married couple. Holly-jolly thanks to the following:

First and foremost, to our beloved friend and editor, Lonnie Hull DuPont. That this book even exists is thanks to you. We appreciate your gracious generosity in giving us YOUR idea and letting us run with it and put our own personal Christmas seal on it while cheering us on all the way. You're the best!

Deepest gratitude to Stephanie Grace Whitson for her touching, heartfelt, and wonderfully written "The First One without Dad" story in the Away in a Ski Lodge chapter. And what a treat as a result, to discover your wonderful novels, including *Walks the Fire*. It's an honor to have your beautiful words in our book.

Special jingle-bell thanks to the entire Jameson family and our new nephew-in-law, Jason Damron, who helped us brainstorm the lyrics to the "God Rest Ye Grumpy Scroogeymen" song. Jason, you're a great and talented addition to the family!

171

Warm-from-the-oven gratitude to Mom for reading an early draft of the book and catching some Norwegian and Danish cooking mistakes. Mange Takk.

Sincere thanks to all the talented folks at Baker/Revell who bring my (now our) books to such wonderful life—from editing to design to sales and marketing and publicity. It's a privilege to be part of the Revell family.

We'd also like to thank everyone who contributed their Christmas tidbits or helped jog our memories on Christmases past as needed: Alan Almeida, Kim Benbow, Curt and Peggy Clark, Jan and Carl Coleman, Debbie Cullifer, Betty Curtis, Jennie and Jason Damron, Joe and Lonnie DuPont, Bettie Eichenberg, Rebecca Fong, Kyle and Lesley Gleve, Kendra Helton, Jim and Sharon and Scott Hetland, Marian Hitchings, Sheri Jameson, Kari Jameson, Laurie Kehler, Pat McLatchey, Diane Melick, John Plastow, Mike and Debbie Rothermel, Char Roushia, Michelle Skinner, David and Patricia Smith, Al and Dolores Souza, Adelaide Thomas, Linda Wright, Lana Yarbrough, Katie Young.

Merry Christmas!

Notes

1. Ace Collins, *Stories behind the Best-Loved Songs of Christmas* (Grand Rapids: Zondervan, 2001), 138. Used by permission.

2. John R. Plastow, *The King's Celebration of Christmas* (Sacramento, Calif.: Plastow Publications, 1994). Used by permission.

3. Barbara Robinson, *The Best Christmas Pageant Ever* (Wheaton, Ill.: Tyndale, 1982), 1.

Laura Jensen Walker is the author of several humor books, including *Dated Jekyll, Married Hyde; Love Handles for the Romantically Impaired; Thanks for the Mammogram!; Mentalpause;* and *Through the Rocky Road and into the Rainbow Sherbet.* A popular speaker and breast cancer survivor, she knows firsthand the healing power of laughter.

Michael Walker, Laura's Renaissance-man husband, works for a major technology company and is a former professional actor and singer. An artist at heart, Michael's passions include public speaking, quilting, and oil painting. With this book he adds "author" to his list of titles. Laura and Michael have a laughter-filled home in Northern California, which they share with their piano-playing dog, Gracie.

For information on having Laura or Michael Walker speak at your event, please contact them through Laura's web site, www.laurajensenwalker.com. To write either of the Walkers, please e-mail them through the web site or write to them at P.O. Box 601325, Sacramento, CA 95680.